MICROSCOPY HANDBOOKS 19

CW00571983

Introduction to Crystallc

REVISED EDITION

C. Hammond

School of Materials, University of Leeds

Oxford University Press · Royal Microscopical Society · 1992

Oxford University Press, Walton Street, Oxford OX2 6DP

Oxford New York Toronto
Delhi Bombay Calcutta Madras Karachi
Petaling Jaya Singapore Hong Kong Tokyo
Nairobi Dar es Salaam Cape Town
Melbourne Auckland

and associated companies in
Berlin Ibadan

Royal Microscopical Society
37/38 St Clements
Oxford OX4 1AJ

Oxford is a trade mark of Oxford University Press

Published in the United States
by Oxford University Press, New York

First edition published 1990
Revised edition published 1992

British Library Cataloguing in Publication Data

Hammond, C.
Introduction to crystallography.
1. Crystallography
I. Title II. Series
548
ISBN 0-19-856433-3

Library of Congress Cataloging in Publication Data

Hammond, C. (Christopher), 1942–
Introduction to crystallography/C. Hammond.
(Microscopy handbooks; 19)
Includes bibliographical references.
1. Crystallography. I. Title. II. Series.
QD905.2.H36 1990 89–22835 548—dc19
ISBN 0-19-856433-3

Typeset by Cotswold Typesetting Ltd, Gloucester
Printed and Bound in Great Britain by
Courier International Limited, East Kilbride

Preface and Acknowledgements

Crystallography is a very simple subject and, for a microscopist, it is a very useful one. It not only provides the basis for a clear understanding of the nature of crystalline specimens, but is also required in order to understand the geometry of diffraction, and therefore the mechanisms of image formation in both the light and electron microscopes. For the microscopist, crystallographic concepts are also essential to an understanding of the electrical or mechanical properties of materials, i.e. topics such as piezo-electricity or deformation mechanisms.

Unfortunately, crystallography is often regarded as an abstruse and 'difficult' subject because it is not easy to learn by the piecemeal accumulation of facts—some guidance and direction are necessary. It is hoped that this handbook will fulfil this tutorial role by taking a reader step-by-step through the basic concepts, avoiding matters of detail or secondary importance. In computer jargon, the handbook is designed to be 'user-friendly'. In addition, models are of great value in understanding the architecture of crystals. They may be constructed of ping-pong balls, hard plastic or expanded polystyrene balls, and throughout the handbook simple model-building exercises are described to supplement the (two-dimensional) diagrams. Appendix 1 gives a list of items which are useful in making up a 'crystallography kit' and the names and addresses of suppliers.

A rapidly increasing number of crystallography programs are becoming available for use with home microcomputers. These programs are either based upon the 'programmed learning' method, which requires a student to respond to questions, or utilize computer graphics to illustrate the change in appearance of objects when viewed from different angles. Details are given in Appendix 2. Appendix 3 gives brief biographical details of some eminent crystallographers whose names are asterisked in the text where they first appear, and in Appendix 4 some useful geometrical relationships are listed.

The handbook is planned in the following way. In Chapter 1 simple crystal structures are described, particular emphasis being placed, by the use of models, on the relationships between them. It is then shown how more complex crystal structures may be built up by, say, introducing small atoms into the gaps of interstices between larger ones. Although this treatment is necessarily brief, it is hoped that the student will understand that the crystal structures of different compounds do not arise in an arbitrary manner, but arise naturally as a result of atomic size and other considerations such as valency and electrical neutrality.

In Chapter 2 the concepts of the lattice and the motif are introduced—concepts which apply to any repeating pattern, not just the three-dimensional patterns of atoms in crystals. These concepts are therefore explained in terms of simple two-dimensional patterns such as the designs seen in wallpapers or fabrics. The concept of symmetry is then introduced and it is shown that its application to two-dimensional patterns leads to what might be thought the surprising conclusion that the number of different types of patterns is very limited: there are only seventeen patterns (known as plane groups), which are based upon only five two-dimensional lattices—oblique, rectangular, hexagonal, square and rhombic (or diamond).

Once the reader has mastered these concepts in two dimensions, the extension to three dimensions should present no difficulties. In Chapters 3 and 4 the fourteen three-dimensional (Bravais) lattices—which constitute the underlying geometrical framework of crystal structures—and the consequent division of crystals into seven systems, are described. In three dimensions it is also shown how many more different types of pattern and additional symmetry elements are possible.

In the past the unambiguous description of crystal planes, faces and directions presented problems, but nowadays 'shorthand' symbols (Miller indices and zone axis symbols) have replaced such long and clumsy (though impressive) phrases as 'trigonal prism of the second order' or 'hemimorphic hexagonal pyramid'. These indices and symbols, the geometrical relationships between them, and particularly the concept of a zone, are covered in Chapter 5.

In Chapter 6 the concept of the reciprocal lattice is introduced and its application to an understanding of the geometry of crystals is explained. This handbook attempts to avoid the frequent difficulties which arise when students are introduced to this concept for the first time, by showing that it can be regarded as a natural development—even a simplification—of the idea of representing lattice planes in crystals; each lattice plane is represented by a vector and the 'end points' of the vectors, all drawn from a common origin, form a lattice—the reciprocal lattice. The formalism of reciprocal lattice vector notation which should not give readers, even with only a little knowledge of vectors, any difficulty, can then be seen as a convenient and elegant shorthand, which follows naturally from a simple geometrical idea. In short, understanding the reciprocal lattice is no more difficult than understanding negative numbers. As the reciprocal lattice of a crystal represents, in effect, lattice planes, its most important applications are in the fields of X-ray and electron diffraction. These are topics for a future handbook. However, the reciprocal lattice vector notation allows many useful geometrical relationships in crystals to be derived very easily. Some such relationships are derived in Chapter 6 and are summarized in Appendix 4. To non-mathematical readers, this part of Chapter 6 may appear to be difficult. Be assured that it is not—it is only unfamiliar!

The author wishes to thank his colleagues, in particular Dr P. M. Kelly and Dr R. Shuttleworth (formerly of the Department of Metallurgy, University of Leeds), for their instruction and guidance; and generations of students for their criticisms, constructive and otherwise, of his teaching methods. Thanks are also due to Mrs J. Nathan for typing the manuscript, to Mr D. Horner for preparing the photographic illustrations, to the copyright holders of several figures as acknowledged in the figure captions, and finally to Dr P. E. Champness and Dr G. W. Lorimer of the University of Manchester/UMIST, who read the typescript, pointed out errors and ambiguities, and offered very many constructive suggestions.

As a result, the author hopes that this handbook does not now contain any ambiguous, disconnected or uncoordinated material, which can so easily mystify or irritate the conscientious and careful reader. He therefore asks that any such material be brought to his attention.

University of Leeds   C.H.
1989

Preface to the revised edition

In response to many suggestions, this revised edition includes an additional chapter (Chapter 7) on the diffraction of light, X-rays and electrons and a brief introduction to the applications of the reciprocal lattice in the analysis of diffraction patterns. An additional appendix (Appendix 5) is a simple introduction to vector nomenclature and analysis for those readers with little mathematical background. It is hoped that these additions will increase the usefulness of the handbook, particularly as an introduction to X-ray and electron diffraction topics covered in more generalized texts.

Thanks are again due to Drs Champness and Shuttleworth and Professor Lorimer, for their very helpful and constructive criticisms of the draft text, to Dr R. F. Cochrane of the School of Materials, University of Leeds and Dr K. M. Crennell of the Rutherford Appleton Laboratory, Didcot, for advice on computer programs, and to Miss Susan Toon of the School of Materials, University of Leeds, for typing the manuscript.

University of Leeds   C.H.
January 1992

Safety

Attention to safety aspects is an integral part of all laboratory procedures and both the Health and Safety at Work Act 1974 and the Control of Substances Hazardous to Health Regulations 1988 impose legal requirements on those persons planning or carrying out such procedures.

In this and other handbooks every effort has been made to ensure that the recipes, formulae, and practical procedures are accurate and safe. However, it remains the responsibility of the reader to ensure that any procedures which are followed are carried out in a safe and competent manner and in compliance with the requirements under the COSHH regulations. Any specific safety instructions relating to items of laboratory equipment must be observed.

Contents

1 Crystals and crystal structures

1.1 The nature of the crystalline state

The beautiful hexagonal patterns of snowflakes, the plane faces and hard faceted shapes of minerals and the bright cleavage fracture surfaces of brittle iron have long been recognized as external evidence of an internal order. However, the nature of this internal order, or the form and scale of the underlying building blocks, was unknown. The first connection between external form or shape of a crystal (or **crystal habit**) and internal structure was made by Robert Hooke* who, with remarkable insight, suggested that the different shapes of crystals which occur—rhombs, trapezia, hexagons, etc.—could arise from the packing together of spheres or globules. Figure 1.1 is 'Scheme VII' from his book *Micrographia*, first published in 1665. The upper part (Fig. 1) is his drawing, from the microscope, of 'Crystalline or Adamantine bodies' occurring on the surface of a cavity in a piece of broken flint and the lower part (Fig. 2) is of 'sand or gravel' crystallized out of urine, which consists of 'Slats or such-like plated Stones . . . their sides shaped into **Rhombs**, **Rhomboeids** and sometimes into **Rectangles** and **Squares**'. He goes on to show how these various shapes can arise from the packing together of 'a company of bullets' as shown in the inset sketches A–L, which represent pictures of crystal structures which have been repeated in innumerable books, with very little variation, ever since. The notion that the packing of the underlying building blocks determines both the shapes of crystals and the angular relationships between the faces was extended by René Just Haüy*. In 1784 Haüy showed how the different forms (or habits) of dog-tooth spar (calcite) could be precisely described by the packing together of little rhombs which he called 'molécules intégrantes' (Fig. 1.2). Thus the connection between an internal order and an external symmetry was established. What was not realized at the time was that an internal order could exist even though there may appear to be no external evidence for it.

It is only relatively recently, as a result primarily of X-ray and electron diffraction techniques, that it has been realized that most materials, including biological materials, are crystalline or partly so. But the notion that a lack of external crystalline form implies a lack of internal regularity still persists. For example, when iron and steel become embrittled there is a marked change in the fracture surface from a rough, irregular 'grey' appearance to a bright faceted 'brittle' appearance. The change in properties from tough to brittle

*Denotes biographical notes available in Appendix 3.

1

Fig. 1.1. 'Scheme VII' (from Hooke's *Micrographia*, 1665), showing crystals in a piece of broken flint (Upper—Fig. 1), crystals from urine (Lower—Fig. 2) and hypothetical sketches of crystal structures A–L arising from the packing together of 'bullets'.

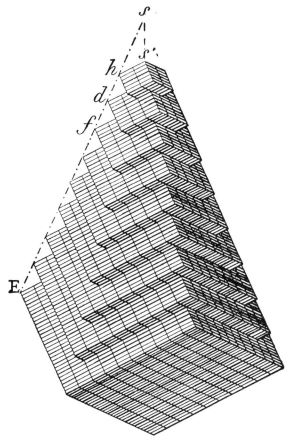

Fig. 1.2. Haüy's representation of dog-tooth spar built up from rhombohedral 'molécules intégrantes' (from *Essai d'une théorie sur la structure des cristaux*, 1784).

is sometimes vaguely thought to arise because the structure of the iron or steel has changed from some undefined amorphous or non-crystalline 'grey' state to a 'crystallized' state. In both situations, of course, the crystalline structure of iron is unchanged; it is simply the fracture processes that are different.

Given our more detailed knowledge of matter we can now interpret Hooke's spheres or 'bullets' as atoms or ions, and Figure 1.1 indicates the ways in which some of the simplest crystal structures can be built up. This representation of atoms as spheres does not, and is not intended, to show anything about their physical or chemical nature. The diameters of the spheres merely express their nearest distances of approach. It is true that these will depend upon the ways in which the atoms are packed together, and whether or not the atoms are ionized, but these considerations do not invalidate the 'hard sphere' model, which is justified, not as a representation of the *structure* of atoms, but as a representation of the structures arising from the *packing together* of atoms.

Consider again Hooke's sketches A–L (Fig. 1.1). In all of these, except the last, L, the atoms are packed together *in the same way*; the differences in shape arise from the different crystal boundaries. The atoms are packed in a *close-packed hexagonal* or honeycomb arrangement—the most compact way which is possible. By contrast, in the *square* arrangement of L there are larger voids or gaps (properly called **interstices**) between the atoms. This difference is shown more clearly in Figure 1.3, where the boundaries of the (two-dimensional) crystals have been left deliberately irregular to emphasize the point that it is the internal regularity, hexagonal or square, not the boundaries (or external faces) which defines the structure of a crystal.

Now we shall extend these ideas to three dimensions by considering not one, but many, layers of atoms, stacked one on top of the other. To understand better the figures which follow, it is very helpful to make models of these layers (Fig. 1.3) to construct the three-dimensional crystal models (see Appendix 1).

Fig. 1.3. Layers of 'atoms' stacked (a) in hexagonal and (b) in square arrays.

1.2 Constructing crystals from close-packed hexagonal layers of atoms

The simplest way of stacking the layers is to place the atom centres directly above one another. The resultant crystal structure is called the **simple hexagonal structure**. There are, in fact, no examples of elements with this structure because, as the model building shows, the atoms in the second layer tend to slip into the 'hollows' or interstices between the atoms in the layer below. This also accords with energy considerations: unless electron orbital considerations predominate, layers of atoms stacked in this 'close-packed' way generally have the lowest (free) energy and are therefore most stable.

When a third layer is placed upon the second we see that there are two possibilities: when the atoms in the third layer slip into the interstices of the second layer they may either end up directly above the atom centres in the first layer or directly above the unoccupied interstices between the atoms in the first layer.

The geometry may be understood from Fig. 1.4, which shows a plan view of atom layers. A is the first layer (with the circular outlines of the atoms drawn in) and B the second layer (outlines of the atoms not shown for clarity). In the first case the third layer goes directly above the A layer, the fourth layer over the B layer, and so on; the stacking sequence then becomes ABABAB . . . and is called the **hexagonal close-packed (hcp) structure**. The packing of idealized hard spheres predicts a ratio of interlayer atomic spacing to in-layer atomic spacing of $\sqrt{(2/3)}$ and although interatomic forces cause deviations from this ratio, metals such as zinc, magnesium and the low-temperature form of titanium have the hcp structure.

In the second case, the third layer of atoms goes above the interstices marked C and the sequence only repeats at the fourth layer, which goes directly above the first layer. The stacking sequence is now ABCABC . . . and is called the **cubic close-packed (ccp) structure**. Metals such as copper, aluminium, silver and gold and the high-temperature form of iron have this structure. The reader may ask the question: "why is a structure which is made up of a three-layer stacking sequence of hexagonal layers called *cubic* close packed?" The answer lies in the shape of the unit cell, which we shall meet below.

These labels for the layers A, B, C are, of course, arbitrary; they could be called OUP or RMS or any combination of three letters or figures. The

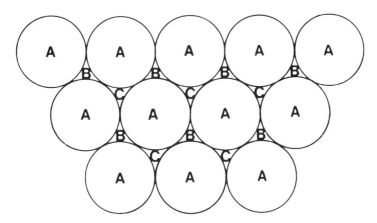

Fig. 1.4. Stacking sequences of close-packed layers of atoms. A—first layer (with outlines of atoms shown); B—second layer; C—third layer.

important point is not the labelling of the layers but their **stacking sequence**; a two-layer repeat for hcp and a three-layer repeat for ccp. Another way of 'seeing the difference' is to notice that in the hcp structure there are open channels perpendicular to the layers running through the connecting interstices (labelled C in Fig. 1.4). In the ccp structure there are no such open channels—they are 'blocked' or obstructed because of the ABCABC ... stacking sequence.

Although the hcp and the ccp are the two most common stacking sequences of close-packed layers, some elements have crystal structures which are 'mixtures' of the two. For example, the actinide element americium has the stacking sequence ABACABAC ... a four-layer repeat which is essentially a combination of an hcp and a ccp stacking sequence. Furthermore, in some elements with nominally ccp or hcp stacking sequences nature sometimes 'makes mistakes' in model building and faults occur during crystal growth or under conditions of stress or deformation. For example, in a (predominantly) ccp crystal (such as cobalt at room temperature), the ABCABC ... (ccp) type of stacking may be interrupted by layers with an ABABAB ... (hcp) type of stacking. The extent of occurrence of these **stacking faults** and the particular combinations of ABCABC ... and ABABAB ... sequences which may arise depend again on energy considerations, with which we are not concerned. What is of crystallographic importance is the fact that stacking faults show how one structure (ccp) may be transformed into another (hcp) and vice versa. They can also be used in the representation of more complicated crystal structures (i.e. of more than one kind of atom), as explained in Section 1.6 below.

1.3 Unit cells of the hcp and ccp structures

Now a simple and economical method is needed to represent the hcp and ccp (and of course other) crystal structures. Diagrams showing the stacked layers of atoms with irregular boundaries would obviously look very confused and complicated—the greater the number of atoms which have to be drawn, the more complicated the picture. The models need to be 'stripped down' to the fewest numbers of atoms which show the essential structure and symmetry. Such 'stripped-down' models are called the **unit cells** of the structures.

The unit cells of the simple hexagonal and hcp structures are shown in Figure 1.5. The similarities and differences are clear: both structures consist of hexagonal close-packed layers; in the simple hexagonal structure these are stacked directly on top of each other, giving an AAA ... type of sequence, and in the hcp structure there is an interleaving layer nestling in the interstices of the layers below and above, giving an ABAB ... type of sequence.

The unit cell of the ccp structure is not so easy to see. There are, in fact, two possible unit cells which may be identified, a cubic cell described below

Fig. 1.5. Unit cells (a) of the simple hexagonal and (b) hcp structures.

(Fig. 1.6), which is almost invariably used, and a smaller rhombohedral cell (Fig. 1.7). Figure 1.6(a) shows three close-packed layers separately—two triangular layers of six atoms (identical to one of Hooke's sketches in Fig. 1.1)—and a third layer stripped down to just one atom. If we stack these layers in an ABC sequence, the result is as shown in Figure 1.6(b): it is a cube with the bottom corner atom missing. This can now be added and the unit cell of the ccp structure, with atoms at the corners and centres of the faces, emerges. The unit cell is usually drawn in the 'upright' position of Figure 1.6(c), and this helps to illustrate a very important point which may have already been spotted whilst model building with the close-packed layers. The close-packed layers lie perpendicular to the body diagonal of the cube, but as there are four different body diagonal directions in a cube, there are therefore four different sets of close-packed layers—not just the one set with which we started. Thus three further close-packed layers have been automatically generated by the ABCABC . . . stacking sequence. This does not occur in the hcp structure—try it and see! The cubic unit cell, therefore, shows the **symmetry** of the ccp structure, a topic which will be covered in Chapter 4. The alternative rhombohedral unit cell of the ccp structure may be obtained by 'stripping away' atoms from the cubic cell such that there are only eight atoms left—one at each of the eight corners—or it may be built up by stacking triangular layers of only three atoms instead of six (Fig. 1.7). Unlike the larger cell, this does not obviously reveal the cubic symmetry of the structure and so is much less useful.

1.4 Constructing crystals from square layers of atoms

It will be noticed that the atoms in the cube faces of the ccp structure lie in a square array like that in Figure 1.3(b) and the ccp structure may be constructed by stacking these layers such that alternate layers lie in the square

Fig. 1.6. Construction of the cubic unit cell of the ccp structure: (a) shows three close-packed layers A, B and C which are stacked in (b) in the 'ABC ...' sequence from which emerges the cubic unit cell which is shown in (c) in the conventional orientation.

interstices marked X in Figure 1.8(a). The models show how the four close-packed layers arise like the faces of a pyramid [Fig. 1.8(b)]. If, on the other hand, the layers are all stacked directly on top of each other, a **simple cubic structure** is obtained [Fig. 1.8(c)]. This is an uncommon structure for the same reason as the simple hexagonal one is uncommon. An example of an element with a simple cubic structure is α-polonium.

1.5 Constructing body-centred cubic crystals

The important and commonly occurring **body-centred cubic (bcc)** structure differs from those already discussed in that it cannot be constructed either from hexagonal close-packed or square-packed layers of atoms (Fig. 1.3). The unit cell of the bcc structure is shown in Figure 1.9. Notice how the body-centring atom 'pushes' the corner ones apart so that, on the basis of the

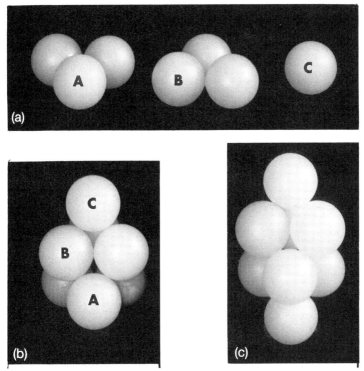

Fig. 1.7. Construction of the rhombohedral unit cell of the ccp structure: the close-packed layers (a) are again stacked (b) in the 'ABC . . .' sequence but the resulting rhombohedral cell (c) does not reveal the cubic symmetry.

'hard sphere' model of atoms discussed above, they are not 'in contact' along the edges [in comparison with the simple cubic structure of Figure 1.8(c), where they are in contact]. In the bcc structure the atoms are in contact only along the body-diagonal directions. The planes in which the atoms are most (not fully) closely packed is the face-diagonal plane, as shown in Figure 1.9(a), and in plan view, showing more atoms, in Figure 1.9(b). The atom centres in the next layer go over the interstices marked B, then the third layer goes over the first layer, and so on—an ABAB . . . type of stacking sequence. The interstices marked B have a slight 'saddle' configuration, and model building will suggest that the atoms in the second layer might slip a small distance to one side or the other (indicated by arrows), leading to a distortion in the cubic struture. Whether such a situation can arise in real crystals, even on a small scale, is still a matter of debate. Metals such as chromium, molybdenum, the high-temperature form of titanium and the low-tempera-ture form of iron have the bcc structure.

Finally, notice the close similarity between the layers of atoms in Figures 1.3(a) and 1.9(b). With only small distortions, e.g. closing of the gaps in

Fig. 1.8. (a) 'Square' layers of atoms with interstices marked X; (b) stacking the layers so that the atoms fall into these interstices, showing the development of the close-packed layers; (c) stacking the layers directly above one another, showing the development of the simple cubic structure.

Fig. 1.9. (a) Unit cell of the bcc structure, showing a face-diagonal plane in which the atoms are most closely packed; (b) a plan view of this 'closest-packed' plane of atoms; the positions of atoms in alternate layers are marked B. The arrows indicate possible slip directions from these positions.

Figure 1.9(b), the two layers are geometrically identical and some important bcc ⇌ ccp and bcc ⇌ hcp transformations are thought to occur as a result of distortions of this kind. For example, when iron is quenched from its high-temperature form (ccp above 910°C) to transform to its low-temperature (bcc) form, it is found that the set of the close-packed and closest-packed layers and close-packed directions are approximately parallel.

1.6 Interstitial structures

The different stacking sequences of one size of atom discussed in Sections 1.2 and 1.5 are not only useful in describing the crystal structures of many of the elements, but can also be used to describe and explain the crystal structures of a wide range of compounds of two or more elements. In particular, they can be applied to those compounds in which 'small' atoms or cations fit into the interstices between 'large' atoms or anions. The different structures of compounds arise from the different numbers and sizes of interstices which occur in the simple hexagonal, hcp, ccp, simple cubic and bcc structures and also from the ways in which the small atoms or cations distribute themselves among these interstices. These ideas can, perhaps, be best understood by considering the types, sizes and numbers of interstices which occur in the ccp and simple cubic structures.

In the ccp structure there are two types and sizes of interstice into which small atoms or cations may fit. They are best seen by fitting small spheres into the interstices between two close-packed atom layers (Fig. 1.4). Consider an atom in a B layer which fits into the hollow or interstice between three A layer atoms: beneath the B atom is an interstice which is surrounded at equal distances by four atoms—three in the A layer and one in the B layer. These four atoms surround or '**co-ordinate**' the interstice in the shape of a tetrahedron, hence the name **tetrahedral interstice** or **tetrahedral interstitial site**, i.e. where a small interstitial atom or ion may be situated. The position of one such site in the ccp unit cell is shown in Figure 1.10(a) and diagrammatically in Figure 1.10(b).

The other interstices between the A and B layers (Fig. 1.4) are surrounded or co-ordinated by six atoms, three in the A layer and three in the B layer. These six atoms surround the interstice in the shape of an octahedron; hence the name **octahedral interstice** or **octahedral interstitial site**. The positions of several atoms or ions in octahedral sites in a ccp unit cell are shown in Figure 1.11(a) and diagrammatically, showing one octahedral site, in Figure 1.11(b).

In the simple cubic structure [Fig. 1.8(c)] there is an interstice at the centre of the unit cell which is surrounded or co-ordinated by the eight atoms at the corners of the cube [Fig. 1.12(a)], hence the name **cubic interstitial site**. Caesium chloride, CsCl, has this structure, as shown diagrammatically in Figure 1.12(b).

Fig. 1.10. (a) An atom in a tetrahedral interstitial site, $r_X/r_A = 0.225$ within the ccp unit cell and (b) geometry of a tetrahedral site, showing the dimensions of the tetrahedron in terms of the unit cell edge length a (from *The Structure of Metals* (3rd edn), by C. S. Barrett and T. B. Massalski, Pergamon, 1980).

Fig. 1.11. (a) Atoms or ions in some of the octahedral interstitial sites, $r_X/r_A = 0.414$ within the ccp unit cell and (b) geometry of an octahedral site, showing the dimensions of the octahedron in terms of the unit cell edge length a (from Barrett and Massalski, *loc. cit.*).

Now the diameters, or radii, of atoms or ions which can just fit into these interstices may easily be calculated on the basis that atoms or ions are spheres of fixed diameter—the 'hard sphere' model. The results are usually expressed as a **radius ratio**, r_X/r_A; the ratio of the radius (or diameter) of the interstitial atoms, X, to that of the large atoms, A with which they are in

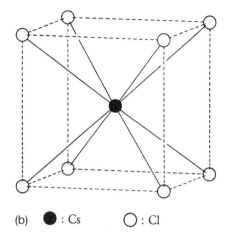

(a)　(b)　● : Cs　○ : Cl

Fig. 1.12. (a) Cubic interstitial site, $r_X/r_A = 0.732$, within the simple cubic unit cell and (b) the CsCl structure (ions not to scale).

contact. In the ccp structure, r_X/r_A for the tetrahedral sites is 0.225 and for the octahedral sites it is 0.414; in the simple cubic structure, r_X/r_A for the cubic sites is 0.732. As well as being of different relative sizes, there are different numbers, or proportions, of these interstitial sites. For both the octahedral sites in ccp, and the cubic sites in the simple cubic structure, the proportion is one interstitial site to one (large) atom or ion, but for the tetrahedral interstitial sites in ccp the proportion is two sites to one atom. These proportions will be evident from model building or, if preferred, by geometrical reasoning. In the simple cubic structure (Fig. 1.12) there is one interstice per unit cell (at the centre) and eight atoms at each of the eight corners. As each corner atom or ion is 'shared' by seven other cells, there is therefore one atom per cell—a ratio of 1:1. In the unit cell of the ccp structure (Fig. 1.11), the octahedral sites are situated at the midpoints of each edge and in the centre. As each edge is shared by three other cells there are four octahedral sites per cell, i.e. twelve edges divided by four (number shared) plus one (centre). There are also four atoms per cell, i.e. eight corners divided by eight (number shared) plus six faces divided by two (number shared), again giving a ratio of 1:1. The tetrahedral sites in the ccp structure (Fig. 1.10) are situated between a corner and three face-centring atoms, i.e. eight tetrahedral sites per unit cell, giving a ratio of 1:2.

It is a useful exercise to determine also the types, sizes and proportions of interstitial sites in the hcp, bcc and simple hexagonal structures. The hcp structure presents no problem; for the 'hard sphere' model with an interlayer to in-layer atomic ratio of $\sqrt{(2/3)}$ (Section 1.2) the interstitial sites are identical to those in ccp. It is only the distribution or 'stacking sequence' of the sites, like that of the close-packed layers of atoms, which is different. In the bcc structure there are octahedral sites at the centres of the faces and mid-parts of the edges [Figs 1.13(a) and (b)] and tetrahedral sites situated between the centres of the faces and mid-points of each edge [Figs 1.13(c) and (d)]. Note, however, that both the octahedron and tetrahedron of the co-ordinating atoms do not have edges of equal length. The octahedron, for example, is 'squashed' in one direction and two of the co-ordinating atoms are closer to the centre of the interstice than are the other four. The radius ratios for the octahedral and tetrahedral interstitial sites are 0.154 and 0.291 respectively.

The radius ratios of interstitial sites and their proportions provide a very rough guide in interpreting the crystal structures of some simple, but important, compounds. The first problem, however, is that the 'radius' of an atom is not a fixed quantity but depends on its state of ionization (i.e. upon the nature of the chemical bonding in a compound) and co-ordination (the number and type of the surrounding atoms or ions). For example, the atomic radius of Li is about 156 pm but the ionic radius of the Li^+ cation is about 60 pm. The atomic radius of Fe in the ccp structure, where each atom is surrounded by twelve others, is about 258 pm but that in the bcc structure, where each atom is surrounded by eight others, is about 248 pm—a contraction in going from twelve- to eight-fold co-ordination of about 4 per cent.

Metal hydrides, nitrides, borides, carbides, etc., in which the radius ratio of the (small) non-metallic or metalloid atoms to the (large) metal atoms is small, provide good examples of interstitial compounds. However, in almost all of these compounds the interstitial atoms are 'oversize' (in terms of the exact radius ratios) and so, in effect, 'push apart' or separate the surrounding atoms such that they are no longer strictly close-packed although their pattern or distribution remains unchanged. For example, Figure 1.14(a) shows the structure of TiN; the nitrogen atoms occupy all the octahedral interstitial sites and, because they are oversize, the titanium atoms are separated but still remain situated at the corners and face centres of the unit cell. This is described as a **face-centred cubic (fcc) array**, rather than a ccp array of titanium atoms, and TiN is described as a **face-centred cubic structure**. This description also applies to all compounds in which some of the atoms occur at the corners and face centres of the unit cell. The ccp structure may therefore be regarded as a special case of the fcc structure in which the atoms are in contact along the face diagonals.

In TiH_2 [Fig. 1.14(b)], the titanium atoms are also in an fcc array and the hydrogen atoms occupy all the tetrahedral sites, the ratio being of course 1:2. In TiH [Fig. 1.14(c)] the hydrogen atoms are again situated in the tetrahedral sites, but only half of these sites are occupied.

Although, as mentioned in Section 1.2, no elements have the simple hexagonal structure in which the close-packed layers are stacked in an AAA ... sequence directly on top of one another [Fig. 1.5(a)], the metal atoms in some metal carbides, nitrides, borides, etc., are stacked in this way,

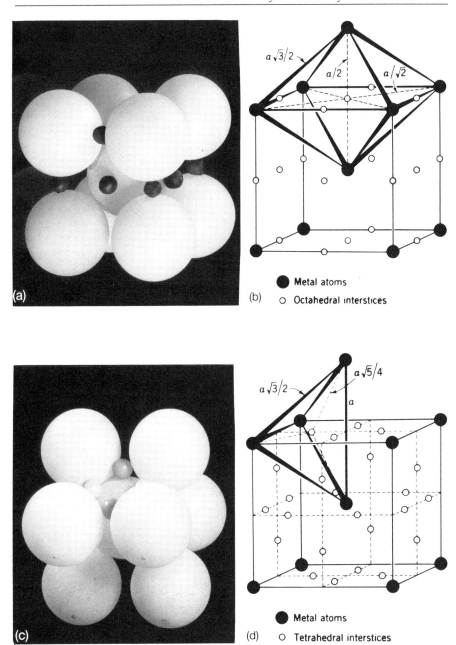

Fig. 1.13. (a) Octahedral interstitial sites, $r_X/r_A = 0.291$, (b) geometry of the octahedral interstitial sites, (c) tetrahedral interstitial sites $r_X/r_A = 0.154$, and (d) geometry of the tetrahedral interstitial sites in the bcc structure. (b) and (d) show the dimensions of the octahedron and tetrahedron in terms of the unit cell edge length a (from Barrett and Massalski, *loc. cit.*).

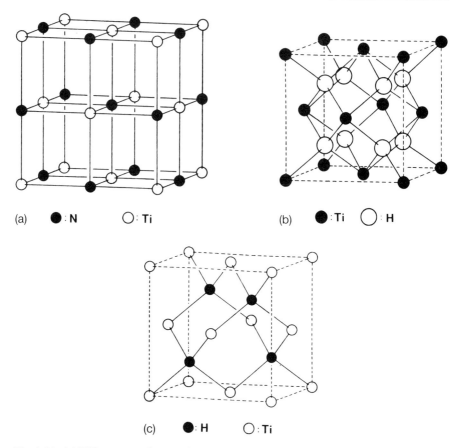

(a)   ● : N   ○ : Ti   (b)   ● : Ti   ○ : H

(c)   ● : H   ○ : Ti

Fig. 1.14. (a) TiN structure (isomorphous with NaCl), (b) TiH$_2$ (isomorphous with CaF$_2$) and (c) TiH structure (isomorphous with sphalerite or zinc blende, ZnS) (from *An Introduction to Crystal Chemistry* (2nd edn), by R. C. Evans, Cambridge University Press, 1964).

the carbon, nitrogen, boron, etc., atoms being situated in some or all of the interstices between the metal atoms. The interstices are half-way between the close-packed (or nearly close-packed) layers and are surrounded or co-ordinated by six atoms—not, however, in the form of an octahedron but in the form of a triangular prism. In the AlB$_2$ structure all these sites are occupied [Fig. 1.15(a)] and in the WC structure only half are occupied [Fig. 1.15(b)].

1.7 Some simple ionic and covalent structures

The ideas presented in Section 1.6 above can be used to describe and explain the crystal structures of many simple but important ionic and covalent compounds, in particular many metal halides, sulphides and oxides.

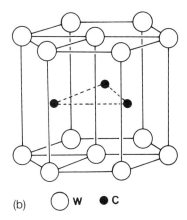

(a) ◯ Al ● B   (b) ◯ W ● C

Fig. 1.15. (a) AlB$_2$ structure, (b) WC structure.

Although the metal atoms or cations are smaller than the chlorine, oxygen, sulphur, etc. atoms or anions, radius ratio considerations are only one factor in determining the crystal structures of ionic and covalent compounds and they are not usually referred to as interstitial compounds even though the pattern or distribution of atoms in the unit cells may be exactly the same. For example, the TiN structure [Fig. 1.14(a)] is isomorphous with the NaCl structure and TiN is isomorphous with NaCl. Similarly, the TiH$_2$ structure [Fig. 1.14(b)] is identical to the Li$_2$O structure and the TiH structure [Fig. 1.14(c)] is isomorphous with the ZnS (zinc blende or sphalerite) structure.

The differences in stacking sequence discussed in Sections 1.2 and 1.6 also explain the different crystal structures or different crystalline polymorphs sometimes shown by one compound. As mentioned above, zinc blende has an fcc structure, the sulphur atoms being stacked in the ABCABC ... sequence. In wurtzite, the other crystal structure or polymorph of zinc sulphide, the sulphur atoms are stacked in the hexagonal ABABAB ... sequence, giving a hexagonal structure. In both cases the zinc atoms occupy half the tetrahedral interstitial sites between the sulphur atoms. As in the case of cobalt, stacking faults may arise during crystal growth or under conditions of deformation, giving rise to 'mixed' sphalerite–wurtzite structures.

Examples of ionic structures based on the simple cubic packing of anions are CsCl and CaF$_2$ (fluorite). In CsCl all the cubic interstitial sites are occupied by caesium cations [Fig. 1.12(b)] but in fluorite only half the sites are occupied by the calcium cations. The resulting unit cell is not just one simple cube of fluorine anions, but a larger cube with a cell side double that of the simple cube and containing therefore $2 \times 2 \times 2 = 8$ cubes, four of which contain calcium cations and four of which are empty.

The distribution of the small calcium cations in the cubic sites is such that they form an fcc array and the fluorite structure can be represented alternatively as an fcc array of calcium cations with all the tetrahedral sites occupied by fluorine anions. It is identical, in terms of the distribution of ionic sites, to the structure of TiH_2 or Li_2O [Fig. 1.14(b)], except that the positions of the cations and anions are reversed; hence Li_2O is said to have the *anti*fluorite structure. However, these differences, although in principle quite simple, may not be clear until we have some better method of representing the atom/ion positions in crystals other than the sketches (or clinographic projections) used in Figures 1.10–1.15.

1.8 Representing crystals in projection: crystal plans

The more complicated the crystal structure and the larger the unit cell, the more difficult it is to visualize the atom or ion positions from diagrams or photographs of models—atoms or ions may be hidden behind others and therefore not seen. Another form of representation, the **crystal plan** or **crystal projection**, is needed, which shows precisely the atomic or ionic positions in the unit cell. The first step is to specify axes x, y and z from a common origin and along the sides of the cell (see Chapter 5). By convention the 'back left-hand corner' is chosen as the origin, the z-axis 'upwards', the y-axis to the right and the x-axis 'forwards', out of the page. The atomic/ionic positions or co-ordinates in the unit cell are specified as fractions of the cell edge lengths in the order x, y, z. Thus in the bcc structure the atomic/ionic co-ordinates are (000) (the atom/ion at the origin) and $(\frac{1}{2}\frac{1}{2}\frac{1}{2})$ (the atom/ion at the centre of the cube). As all eight corners of the cube are *equivalent positions* (i.e. any of the eight corners can be chosen as the origin), there is no need to write down atomic/ionic co-ordinates (100), (110), etc.; (000) specifies *all* the corner atoms, and the two co-ordinates (000) and $(\frac{1}{2}\frac{1}{2}\frac{1}{2})$ are equal to the two atoms/ions in the bcc unit cell. In fcc, with four atoms/ions per unit cell, the co-ordinates are (000), $(\frac{1}{2}\frac{1}{2}0)$, $(\frac{1}{2}0\frac{1}{2})$, $(0\frac{1}{2}\frac{1}{2})$.

Crystal projections or plans are usually drawn perpendicular to the z-axis, and Figures 1.16(a) and (b) are plans of the bcc and fcc structures respectively. Note that only the z co-ordinates are indicated in these diagrams; the x and y co-ordinates need not be written down because they are clear from the plan. Similarly, no z co-ordinates are indicated for all the corner atoms because all eight corners are equivalent positions in the structure, as mentioned above.

Figure 1.16(c) shows a projection of the antifluorite (LiO_2) structure; the oxygen anions in the fcc positions and the lithium cations in all the tetrahedral interstitial sites with z co-ordinates one-quarter and three-quarters between the oxygen anions are clearly shown. Notice that the lithium cations are in a simple cubic array, i.e. equivalent to the fluorine anions in the fluorite structure. The alternative fluorite unit cell, made up of eight simple cubes (see Section 1.7), is drawn by shifting the origin of the axes in Figure 1.16(c)

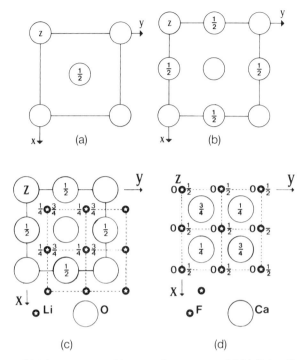

Fig. 1.16. Plans of (a) bcc structure, (b) ccp or fcc structure, (c) Li_2O (antifluorite) structure, (d) CaF_2 (fluorite) structure.

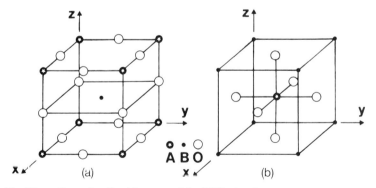

Fig. 1.17. Alternative unit cells of the perovskite ABO_3 structure.

to the ion at the $(\frac{1}{4}\frac{1}{4}\frac{1}{4})$ site and relabelling the co-ordinates. The result is shown in Figure 1.16(d).

Sketching crystal plans helps you to understand the similarities and differences between structures; in fact, it is very difficult to understand them otherwise! For example, Figures 1.17(a) and (b) show the same crystal structure (perovskite, $CaTiO_3$). They look different because the origins of the cells have been chosen to coincide with different atoms/ions.

Exercises

1. Draw crystal plans of the perovskite structure shown in Figure 1.17, relocate the origin of one cell, relabel the ionic co-ordinates and show that these two cells do represent the same crystal structure.

2. With reference to Figures 1.10(b), 1.11(b), 1.13(b) and 1.13(d) (or your crystal models) check the radius ratios stated in the text for the tetrahedral and octahedral interstitial sites in the ccp and bcc structures.
   (*Hint:* These figures show the dimensions of the co-ordination polyhedra in terms of *a*, the cell edge lengths.)

3. Examine your crystal models and find:
   (a) the number of different (non-parallel) close-packed planes and close-packed directions in the ccp and hcp structures; and
   (b) the number of closest-packed planes and close-packed directions in the bcc structure.

4. In the deformation of ccp and bcc metals, slip generally occurs on the close- or closest-packed planes and in close-packed directions. Each combination of slip plane and direction is called a **slip system**. How many slip systems are there in these metals?

5. With reference to Figure 1.5(b), calculate the *c/a* ratio for the hcp structure.
   (*Hint: a* is equal to *d*, the atomic diameter and edge length of the tetrahedron, and *c* is twice the height of the tetrahedron.)

2 Two-dimensional patterns, lattices and symmetry

2.1 Approaches to the study of crystal structures

In Chapter 1 we developed an understanding of simple crystal structures by first considering the ways in which atoms or ions could pack together and then introducing smaller atoms or ions into the interstices between the larger ones. This is a practical approach as it not only provides us with an immediate and straightforward understanding of the atomic/ionic arrangements in some simple compounds, but also suggests the ways in which more complicated compounds can be built up.

However, it is not a systematic and rigorous approach, as all the possibilities of atomic arrangements in all crystal structures are not explored. The rigorous, and essentially mathematical, approach is to analyse and classify the geometrical characteristics of quite general two-dimensional patterns and then to extend the analysis to three dimensions to arrive at a completely general description of all the patterns to which atoms or molecules or groups of atoms or molecules might conform in the crystalline state.

These two distinct approaches—or strands of crystallographic thought—are apparent in the literature of the nineteenth and early twentieth centuries. In general, it was the metallurgists and chemists, such as Tammann* and Pope*, who were the pragmatists, and the theoreticians and geometers, such as Fedorov* and Schoenflies*, who were the analysts. It might be thought that the analytical is necessarily superior to the pragmatic approach because its generality and comprehensiveness provides a much more powerful starting point for progress to be made in the discovery and interpretation of the crystal structures of more and more complex substances. But this is not so. It was, after all, the simple models of sodium chloride and zinc blende of Pope (such as we also constructed in Chapter 1) that helped to provide the Braggs* with the necessary insight into crystal structures to enable them to make their great advances in the interpretation of X-ray diffraction photographs. In the same way, 40 years later, the discovery of the structure of DNA by Watson and Crick was based as much upon structural and chemical knowledge and intuition and model building as upon formal crystallographic theory.

However, a more general appreciation of the different patterns into which

*Denotes biographical notes available in Appendix 3.

atoms and molecules may be arranged is essential, because it leads to an understanding of the important concepts of symmetry, motifs and lattices. The topic need not be pursued rigorously—in fact it is unwise to do so because a student might quickly 'lose sight of the wood for the trees!' The essential ideas can be appreciated in two dimensions, the subject of this chapter. The extension to three dimensions (Chapters 3 and 4) which relates to 'real crystal structures', should then present no conceptual difficulties.

2.2 Two-dimensional patterns and lattices

Consider the pattern of Figure 2.1(a), which is made up of the letter **R** repeated indefinitely. What does **R** represent? Anything you like—a 'two-dimensional molecule', a cluster of atoms or whatever. Representing the 'molecule' as an **R**, an *asymmetric* shape, is in effect representing an *asymmetric* molecule. We shall discuss the different types or elements of symmetry in detail in Section 2.3 below, but for the moment our general everyday knowledge is enough. For example, consider the symmetry of the letters **R M S**. **R** is asymmetrical. **M** consists of two equal sides, each of which is a reflection or mirror image of the other; there is a **mirror line** of symmetry down the centre indicated by the letter m, thus **M**ₘ. There is no mirror line in the **S**, but if it is rotated 180° about a point in its centre, an identical **S** appears; there is a **two-fold rotation axis** usually called a **diad axis** at the centre of the **S**. This is represented by a little lens-shape at the axis of rotation: **S**

In Figure 2.1(a) **R**, the repeating 'unit of pattern' is called the **motif**. These motifs may be considered to be situated at or near the intersections of an (imaginary) grid. The grid is called the **lattice** and the intersections are called **lattice points**.

Let us now draw this underlying lattice in Figure 2.1(a). First we have to decide where to place each lattice point in relation to each motif: anywhere will do—above, below, to one side, in the 'middle' of the motif—the only requirement is that the *same* position with respect to the motif is chosen every time. We shall choose a position a little below the motif, as shown in Figure 2.1(b). Now there are an infinite number of ways in which the lattice points may be 'joined up' (i.e. an infinite number of ways of drawing a lattice

(a)   (b)   (c)

Fig. 2.1. (a) A pattern with the motif **R**, (b) with the lattice points indicated and (c) the lattice and a unit cell outlined.

or grid of lines through lattice points). In practice, a grid is usually chosen which 'joins up' adjacent lattice points to give the lattice as shown in Figure 2.1(c), and a unit cell of the lattice may also be outlined. Clearly, if we know (1) the size and shape of the unit cell and (2) the motif which each lattice point represents, including its orientation with respect to the lattice point, we can draw the whole pattern or build up the whole structure indefinitely. The unit cell of the lattice and the motif therefore define the whole pattern or structure. This is very simple: but observe an important consequence. Each motif is identical and, for an infinitely extended pattern, the environment of each motif is identical. This provides us with the definition of a lattice (which applies equally in two and three dimensions): *a lattice is an array of points in space in which the environment of each point is identical.*

Like all simple definitions (and indeed ideas), this definition of a lattice is often not fully appreciated; there is, to use a colloquial expression, 'more to it than meets the eye!' This is particularly the case when we come to three-dimensional lattices (Chapter 4), but, for the two-dimensional case, consider the patterns of points in Figure 2.2 (which should be thought of as extending infinitely). Of these only (a) and (d) constitute a lattice; in (b) and (c) the points are certainly in a *regular* array, but the surroundings of each point are *not* all identical.

Figures 2.2(a) and (d) represent two two-dimensional lattice types, named **oblique** and **rectangular** respectively in view of the shapes of their unit cells. But what is the distinction between the oblique and rectangular lattices? Surely the rectangular lattice is just a special case of the oblique, i.e. with a 90° angle?

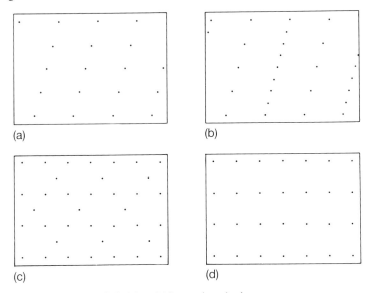

(a)

(b)

(c)

(d)

Fig. 2.2. Patterns of points. Only (a) and (d) constitute lattices.

The distinction arises from different symmetries of the two lattices, and requires us to extend our everyday notions of symmetry and to classify a series of symmetry elements. This precise knowledge of symmetry can then be applied to both the motif and the lattice and will show that there are a limited number of patterns with different symmetries (only seventeen) and a limited number of two-dimensional lattices (only five).

2.3 Two-dimensional symmetry elements

The clearest way of developing the concept of symmetry is to begin with an asymmetrical 'object'—say the **R** of Figure 2.1—then to add successively mirror lines and axes of symmetry and to see how the **R** is repeated to form different patterns of groups. The different patterns or groups of **R**s which are produced correspond, of course, to objects or projections of molecules (i.e. 'two-dimensional molecules') with different symmetries which are not possessed by the **R** alone.

For example, consider Figure 2.3(a). 'Right-' and 'left-'handed **R**s are reflected in the 'vertical' mirror line between them. This pair of **R**s has the

Fig. 2.3. Generation of motifs (a)–(e) with different symmetries (five out of the ten plane point groups) and examples of two-dimensional symbols and (right) molecules and ions. (a) *Cis*-difluoroethene, (b) ethene, (c) *trans*-difluoroethene, (d) trialkylfluoride ammonium ion and (e) carbonate ion.

same mirror symmetry as the letter **M**, or the projection of the *cis*-difluoro-ethene molecule. Now add another 'horizontal' mirror line as in Figure 2.3(b). A group of four **R**s—two right and two left handed—is produced. This group has the same symmetry as the single letter **O** or the projection of the ethene molecule.

The **R** may also be repeated with a diad (two-fold rotation) axis, as in Figure 2.3(c). The two **R**s—both right handed—have the same symmetry as the letter **S** as we saw above, or the *trans*-difluoroethene molecule. Now look back to the group of **R**s in Figure 2.3(b); notice that they are also related by a diad (two-fold rotation axis) at the intersection of the mirror lines: the action of reflecting the **R**s across two perpendicular mirror lines 'automatically' generates the two-fold symmetry as well. This effect, where the action of one symmetry element generates another, is quite general, as we shall see below.

Mirror lines and diad axes of symmetry are just two of the symmetry elements in two dimensions. In addition, there are three-fold, rotation or **triad** axes (represented by a little triangle ▲), four-fold rotation or **tetrad** axes (represented by a little square ■) and six-fold rotation or **hexad** axes (represented by a little hexagon ●). Figure 2.3(d) shows the **R** related by a triad (three-fold) axis. The paper windmill and the projection of the trialkylfluoride ammonium ion also have this same symmetry. Now add a 'vertical' mirror line as in Figure 2.3(e). Three more (left-handed) **R**s are generated, and at the same time, the **R**s are mirror-related not just in the vertical line but also in two lines inclined at 60° as shown, another example of additional symmetry elements—in this case mirror-lines—being automatically generated.

This procedure—of generating groups of **R**s which represent motifs with different symmetries—may be repeated with tetrad (four-fold) and hexad (six-fold) rotation axes of symmetry. Altogether there are ten such symmetries in two dimensions or **ten plane point groups**, so called because all the symmetry elements pass through one point. The ten plane point groups are labelled with 'shorthand' symbols which indicate the symmetry elements present; *m* for one mirror plane, *mm* or *mm*2 for two mirror planes (plus diad), 2 for a diad, 3 for a triad, 3*m* for a triad and three mirror planes and so on. The assiduous reader should complete Figure 2.3 for himself or herself including, as well as the **R**s, common objects and molecules with the appropriate symmetries. In addition, it will become obvious why it is not possible to have five-, seven-, eight , etc., fold rotation axes of symmetry. A five-fold 'pentad' axis, for example, would require five lattice points to be equally arranged about the axis, but such an arrangement of points could not be put together to form a lattice. Try it and see!

2.4 The five plane lattices

Having examined some of the types of symmetry which a two-dimensional

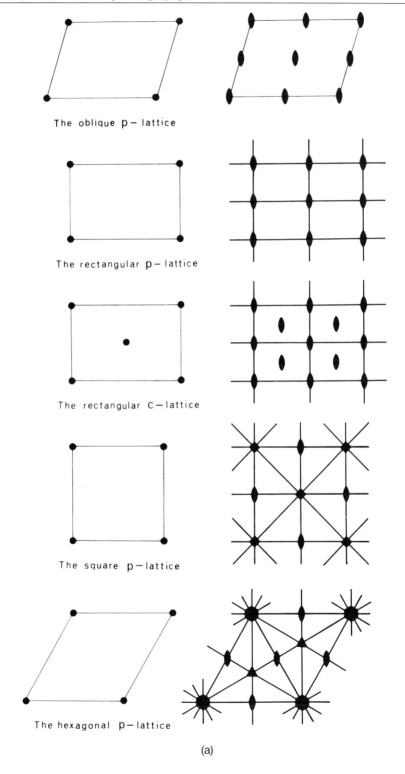

The oblique p−lattice

The rectangular p−lattice

The rectangular C−lattice

The square p−lattice

The hexagonal p−lattice

(a)

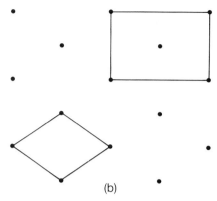

(b)

Fig. 2.4. (a) Unit cells of the five plane lattices, showing (right) the symmetry elements present (from *Essentials of Crystallography*, by D. McKie and C. McKie, Blackwell, 1986). (b) The rectangular *C* lattice, showing the alternative primitive (rhombic *P* or diamond *P*) unit cell.

motif can possess (Fig. 2.3), we can now determine how many two-dimensional or plane lattices there are. The important criterion is this: the lattice itself must possess the symmetry of the motif; it may possess more symmetry elements but it cannot possess fewer. Or, put another way, the symmetry of the arrangement of lattice points around each lattice point must be the same as, or greater than, the symmetry of the motif. A few examples will make this clear. Consider the rectangular lattice of Figure 2.2(d). Through each lattice point and half-way between there are vertical and horizontal lines of symmetry intersecting diad axes. The motif of Figure 2.3(b) also has this symmetry and therefore it follows that a pattern with such a motif will have a rectangular lattice. The motif of Figure 2.3(a) has one mirror line, and a pattern with this motif will also have a rectangular lattice—in this case the symmetry of the lattice is greater than that of the motif. Note, on the other hand, that the motifs with one or two mirror lines of symmetry [Figs 2.3(a) and (b)] cannot occur in a pattern with the oblique lattice because the oblique lattice does not itself have any mirror lines of symmetry.

This procedure can be applied to all the other motifs. For example, a motif with tetrad (four-fold) symmetry applies to a pattern with a square lattice and a motif with triad (three-fold) symmetry [Figs 2.3(d) and (e)] and hexad (six-fold) symmetry will apply to a pattern with an hexagonal lattice. Altogether, five two-dimensional or plane lattices may be worked out, as shown in Figure 2.4(a). They are described by the shapes of the unit cells which are drawn between lattice points—oblique *p*, rectangular *p*, rectangular *c* (which is distinguished from rectangular *p* by having an additional lattice point in the centre of the cell), square *p* and hexagonal *p*.

All two-dimensional patterns must be based upon one of these five plane lattices; no others are possible. This may seem very surprising—surely other shapes of unit cells are possible? The answer is 'yes', a large number of unit cell shapes are possible, but the pattern of lattice points which they describe will be one of the five of Figure 2.4(a). For example, the rectangular *c* lattice may also be described as a rhombic *p* or diamond *p* lattice, depending upon which unit cell is chosen to 'join up' the lattice points [Fig. 2.4(b)]. These are just two alternative descriptions of the *same* arrangement of lattice points. So the choice of unit cell is arbitrary: *any* four lattice points can be joined up to form a unit cell. In practice we take a sensible course and mostly choose a unit cell that is as small as possible—or 'primitive' (symbol *p*)—which does not contain other lattice points within it. Sometimes a larger cell is more useful because the axes joining up the sides are at 90°. Examples are the rhombic or diamond lattice which is identical to the rectangular centred lattice described above and, to take an important three-dimensional case, the cubic cell [Fig. 1.6(c)] which is used to describe the ccp structure in preference to the primitive rhombohedral cell [Fig. 1.7(c)].

Now as there are ten point group symmetries which a motif can possess (five of which are shown in Figure 2.3), it may be thought that there are therefore only ten different types of two-dimensional patterns, distributed among the five plane lattices. However, there is a complication: the combination of a point group symmetry with a lattice can give rise to an additional symmetry element called a **glide line**. Consider the two patterns in Figure 2.5, both of which have a rectangular lattice. In Figure 2.5(a) the motif has mirror symmetry as in Figure 2.3(a); it consists of a pair of right- and left-handed **R**s. In Figure 2.5(b) there is still a reflection—still pairs of right- and left-handed **R**s—but one set of **R**s has been translated, or glided half a lattice spacing. This symmetry is called a **reflection-glide** or simply a **glide line of symmetry**. Notice that glide lines also arise automatically in the centre of the unit cell of Figure 2.5(b) as do mirror lines in Figure 2.5(a).

Glide lines give seven more two-dimensional patterns, giving seventeen in all—the seventeen **plane groups**. On a macroscopic scale the glide symmetry in a crystal would appear as simple mirror symmetry—the shift between the mirror-related parts of the motif would only be observable in an electron microscope which was able to resolve the individual mirror-related parts of the motif, i.e. distances of the order of 0.5–2 Å (50–200 pm).

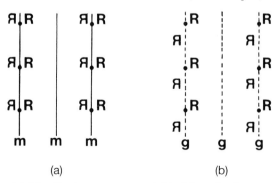

Fig. 2.5. Patterns with (a) reflection symmetry and (b) glide–reflection symmetry. The mirror lines (*m*) and glide lines (*g*) are indicated.

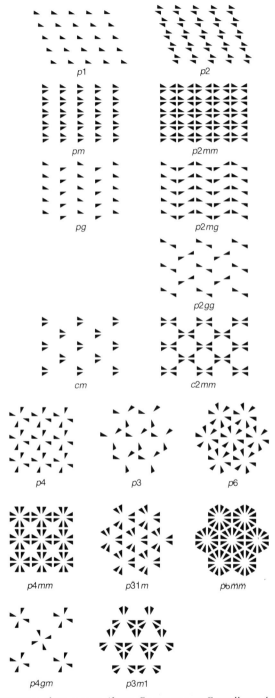

Fig. 2.6. The seventeen plane groups (from *Contemporary Crystallography*, by M. J. Buerger, Wiley, 1963).

The seventeen plane groups are shown in Figure 2.6. They are labelled by 'shorthand' symbols which indicate the type of lattice (*p* for primitive, *c* for centred) and the symmetry elements present, *m* for mirror lines, *g* for glide lines, 4 for tetrads and so on.

It is essential to practice recognizing the motifs, symmetry elements and lattice types in two-dimensional patterns and therefore to find which of the seventeen plane groups they belong. Any regular patterned objects will do—wallpapers, fabric designs, or the examples at the end of this chapter. Figure 2.7 indicates the procedure you should follow. Cover up Figure 2.7(b) and examine only Figure 2.7(a); it is a projection of molecules of $C_6(CH_3)_4$. Recognize that the molecules or groups of atoms are *not* identical in this projection. The motif is a *pair* of such molecules and this is the 'unit of pattern' that is repeated. Now look for symmetry elements and (using a piece of tracing paper) indicate the positions of all of these on the pattern. Compare your pattern of symmetry elements with those shown in Figure 2.7(b). If you did not obtain the same result you have not been looking carefully enough! Finally, insert the lattice points—one for each motif. Anywhere will do, but it is convenient to have them coincide with a symmetry element, as has been done in Figure 2.7(b). The lattice is clearly oblique and the plane group is *p*2 (see Figure 2.6).

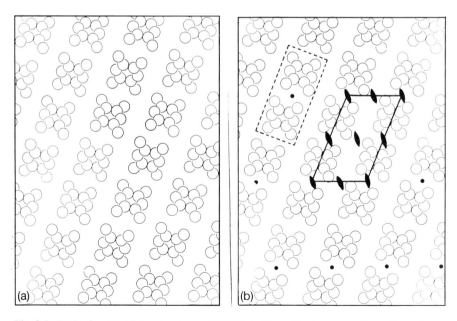

Fig. 2.7. Projection (a) of the structure of $C_6(CH_3)_4$ (from *Contemporary Crystallography*, by M. J. Buerger, McGraw-Hill, 1970) with (b) the motif, lattice and symmetry elements indicated.

Exercises

1. Lay tracing paper over the plane patterns in Figure 2.6. Outline a unit cell in each case and indicate the positions of all the symmetry elements within the unit cell. Notice in particular the differences in the distribution of the triad axes and mirror lines in the plane groups $p31m$ and $p3m1$.
2. Figure 2.8 is a design by M. C. Escher. Using a tracing paper overlay, indicate the positions of all the symmetry elements. What is the plane lattice type?

Fig. 2.8. A plane pattern (from *Symmetry Aspects of M. C. Escher's Periodic Drawings* (2nd edn), by C. H. MacGillavry, Published for the International Union of Crystallography by Bohn, Scheltema & Holkema, Utrecht, 1976).

3. Figure 2.9 is a design by M. C. Escher. Can you see that the two sets of men are related by glide lines of symmetry? Draw in the positions of these glide lines, and determine the plane lattice type.

Fig. 2.9. A plane pattern (from C. H. MacGillavry, *loc. cit.*).

4. Determine the plane point group symmetry of a chess board (a) without the chessmen and (b) with the chessmen in the opening position (ignore the difference in colour of the chessmen).

3 Bravais lattices and crystal systems

3.1 Introduction

The definitions of the motif—the repeating 'unit of pattern' and the lattice—an array of points in space in which each point has an identical environment—hold in three as in two dimensions. However, in three dimensions there are additional symmetry elements that need to be considered: both **point symmetry elements** to describe the symmetry of the three-dimensional motif (or indeed any crystal or three-dimensional object) and also **translational symmetry elements**, which are required (like glide lines in the two-dimensional case) to describe all the possible patterns which arise by combining motifs of different symmetries with their appropriate lattices. Clearly, these considerations suggest that the subject is going to be rather more complicated and 'difficult'; it is obvious that there are going to be many more three-dimensional patterns (or space groups) than the seventeen two-dimensional patterns (or plane groups—Chapter 2), and to work through all of these systematically would take up many pages! However, it is not necessary to do so; all that is required is an understanding of the principles involved (Chapter 2), the operation and significance of the additional symmetry elements, and the main results. These may be stated straight away. The additional point symmetry elements required are centres of symmetry, mirror planes (instead of lines) and inversion axes; the additional translational symmetry elements are glide planes (instead of lines) and screw axes. The application and permutation of all symmetry elements to patterns in space give rise to 230 **space groups** (instead of seventeen plane groups) distributed among fourteen space lattices (instead of five plane lattices) and thirty-two point group symmetries (instead of ten plane point group symmetries).

In this chapter the concept of space (or Bravais) lattices and their symmetries is discussed and, deriving from this, the classification of crystals into seven systems.

3.2 The fourteen space (Bravais) lattices

The systematic work of describing and enumerating the space lattices was done by Frankenheim* who, in 1835, proposed that there were fifteen in all. Unfortunately for Frankenheim, two of his lattices were identical, a fact first

*Denotes biographical notes available in Appendix 3.

pointed out by Bravais* in 1848. It was, to take a two-dimensional analogy, as if Frankenheim had failed to notice [see Fig. 2.4(b)] that the rhombic or diamond and the rectangular centred plane lattices were identical! Hence, to this day, the fourteen space lattices are usually, and perhaps unfairly, called Bravais lattices.

The unit cells of the Bravais lattices are shown in Figure 3.1. The different shapes and sizes of these cells may be described in terms of three cell edge lengths or axial distances, a, b, c, or lattice vectors $\mathbf{a}$, $\mathbf{b}$, $\mathbf{c}$ and the angles between them, α, β, γ, where α is the angle between $\mathbf{b}$ and $\mathbf{c}$, β the angle between $\mathbf{a}$ and $\mathbf{c}$, and γ the angle between $\mathbf{a}$ and $\mathbf{b}$. The axial distances and angles are usually measured from one corner to the cell, i.e. a common origin. It does not matter where we take the origin—any corner will do—but, as pointed out in Chapter 1, it is a useful convention (and helps to avoid confusion) if the origin is taken as the 'back left-hand corner' of the cell, the a-axis pointing forward (out of the page), the b-axis towards the right and the c-axis upwards. This convention also gives a right-handed axial system. If any one of the axes is reversed (e.g. the b-axis towards the left instead of the right), then a left-handed axial system results. The distinction between them is that, like left and right hands, they are mirror-images of one another and cannot be brought into coincidence by rotation.

The drawings of the unit cells of the Bravais lattices in Figure 3.1 can be misleading because, as shown in Chapter 2, it is the *pattern* of lattice points which distinguishes the lattices. The unit cells simply represent arbitrary, though convenient, ways of 'joining up' the lattice points. Consider, for example, the three cubic lattices; cubic P (for *P*rimitive, one lattice point per cell, i.e. lattice points only at the corners of the cell), cubic I (for '*I*nnenzentrierte', which is German for 'body-centred', an additional lattice point at the centre of the cell, giving two lattice points per cell) and cubic F (for *F*ace-centred, with additional lattice points at the centres of each face of the cell, giving four lattice points per cell). It is possible to outline primitive cells (i.e. lattice points only at the corners) for the cubic I and cubic F lattices, as shown in Figure 3.2. As mentioned in Chapter 1, these primitive cells are not often used (1) because the inter-axial angles are not the convenient 90° (i.e. they are not orthogonal) and (2) because they do not reveal very clearly the cubic symmetry of the cubic I and cubic F lattices. (The symmetry of the Bravais lattices, or rather the point group symmetries of their unit cells, will be described in Section 3.3.)

Similar arguments concerning the use of primitive cells apply to all the other centred lattices. Notice that the unit cells of two of the lattices are centred on the 'top' and 'bottom' faces. These are called base-centred or C-centred because these faces are intersected by the c-axis.

The Bravais lattices may be thought of as being built up by stacking 'layers' of the five plane lattices, one on top of another. The cubic and tetragonal lattices are based on the stacking of square lattice layers; the orthorhombic P and I lattices on the stacking of rectangular layers; the orthorhombic C and F

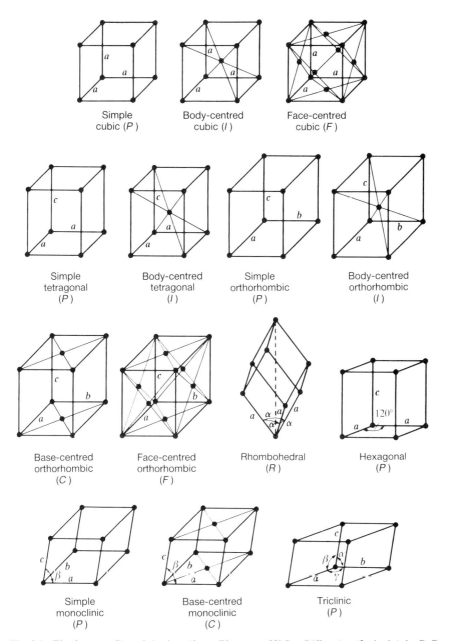

Fig. 3.1. The fourteen Bravais lattices (from *Elements of X-Ray Diffraction* (2nd edn), by B. D. Cullity, Addison–Wesley, 1978).

Fig. 3.2. (a) The cubic *I* and (b) the cubic *F* lattices with the primitive rhombohedral cells and inter-axial angles indicated.

lattices on the stacking of rectangular centred layers; the rhombohedral and hexagonal lattices on the stacking of hexagonal layers and the monoclinic and triclinic lattices on the stacking of oblique layers. These relationships between the plane and the Bravais lattices are easy to see, except perhaps for the rhombohedral lattice. The rhombohedral unit cell has axes of equal length and with equal angles (α) between them. Notice that the layers of lattice points, perpendicular to the 'vertical' direction (shown dotted in Figure 3.1) form triangular, or equivalently, hexagonal layers. The hexagonal and rhombohedral lattices differ in the ways in which the hexagonal layers are stacked. In the hexagonal lattice they are stacked directly one on top of the other [Fig. 3.3(a)] and in the rhombohedral lattice they are stacked such that the next two layers of points lie above the triangular 'hollows' or interstices of the layer below, giving a three layer repeat [Fig. 3.3(b)]. These hexagonal and rhombohedral stacking sequences have been met before in the stacking of close-packed layers (Chapter 1); the hexagonal lattice corresponds to the simple hexagonal AAA ... sequence and the rhombohedral lattice corresponds to the fcc ABCABC ... sequence.

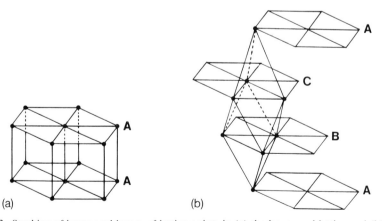

Fig. 3.3. Stacking of hexagonal layers of lattice points in (a) the hexagonal lattice and (b) the rhombohedral lattice.

Now observant readers will notice that the rhombohedral and cubic lattices are therefore related. The primitive cells of the cubic *I* and cubic *F* lattices (Fig. 3.2) are rhombohedral—the axes are of equal length and the angles (α) between them are equal. As in the two-dimensional cases, what distinguishes the cubic lattices from the rhombohedral is their symmetry. When the angle α is 90° we have a cubic *P* lattice, when it is 60° we have a cubic *F* lattice and when it is 109.47° we have a cubic *I* lattice (Fig. 3.2). Or, alternatively, when the hexagonal layers of lattice points in the rhombohedral lattice are spaced apart in such a way that the angle α is 90°, 60° or 109.47°, then cubic symmetry results.

Finally, compare the orthorhombic lattices (all sides of the unit cell of different lengths) with the tetragonal lattices (two sides of the cell of equal length). Why are there four orthorhombic lattices, *P*, *C*, *I* and *F* and only two tetragonal lattices, *P* and *I*? Why are there not tetragonal *C* and *F* lattices as well? The answer is that there *are* tetragonal *C* and *F* lattices, but by redrawing or outlining different unit cells, as shown in Figure 3.4, it will be seen that they are identical to the tetragonal *P* and *I* lattices respectively. In short, they represent no new arrangements of lattice points.

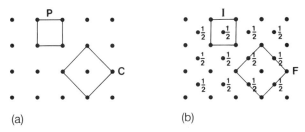

Fig. 3.4. Plans of tetragonal lattices, showing (a) the tetragonal $P = C$ lattice and (b) the tetragonal $I = F$ lattice.

3.3 The symmetry of the fourteen Bravais lattices: crystal systems

The unit cells of the Bravais lattices may be thought of as the 'building blocks' of crystals, precisely as Haüy envisaged (Fig. 1.2). Hence it follows that the habit or external shape, or the observed symmetry of crystals, will be based upon the shapes and symmetry of the Bravais lattices, and we now have to describe the point symmetry of the unit cells of the Bravais lattices just as we described the point symmetry of plane patterns and lattices. The subject is far more readily understood if simple models are used (Appendix 1).

First, mirror lines of symmetry become mirror planes in three dimensions. Second, axes of symmetry (diads, triads, tetrads and hexads) also apply to three dimensions. The additional complication is that, whereas a plane motif or object can only have one such axis (perpendicular to its plane), a three-dimensional object can have several axes running in different directions (but always through a point in the centre of the object).

Consider, for example, a cubic unit cell [Fig. 3.5(a)]. It contains a total of nine mirror planes, three parallel to the cube faces and six parallel to the face diagonals. There are three tetrad (four-fold) axes perpendicular to the three sets of cube faces, four triad (three-fold) axes running between opposite cube corners, and six diad (two-fold) axes running between the centres of opposite edges. This 'collection' of symmetry elements is called the **point group symmetry** of the cube because all the elements—planes and axes—pass through a point in the centre.

Similarly, Figure 3.5(b) shows the point group symmetry of an orthorhombic unit cell. It contains, like the cube, three mirror planes parallel to the faces of the cell but no more—mirror planes do not exist parallel to the face diagonals. The only axes of symmetry are three diads perpendicular to the three faces of the unit cell.

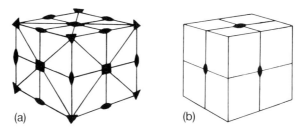

Fig. 3.5. The point symmetry elements in (a) a cube (cubic unit cell) and (b) an orthorhombic prism (orthorhombic unit cell).

In both cases it can be seen that the point group symmetry of these unit cells [Figs 3.5(a) and 3.5(b)] is independent of whether the cells are centred or not. All three cubic lattices, *P, I* and *F*, have the same point group symmetry; all four orthorhombic lattices, *P, I, F* and *C*, have the same point group symmetry and so on. This simple observation leads to an important conclusion: it is not possible, from the observed symmetry of a crystal, to tell whether the underlying Bravais lattice is centred or not. Therefore, in terms of their point group symmetries, the Bravais lattices are grouped, according to the shapes of their unit cells, into seven **crystal systems**. For example, crystals with cubic *P, I* or *F* lattices belong to the **cubic system**, crystals with orthorhombic *P, I, F* or *C* lattices belong to the **orthorhombic system**, and so on. However, a complication arises in the case of crystals with a hexagonal lattice. One might expect that all crystals with a hexagonal lattice should belong to the hexagonal system, but, as shown in Chapter 4, the external symmetry of crystals may not be identical (and usually is not identical) to the symmetry of the underlying Bravais lattice. Some crystals with a hexagonal lattice, e.g. α-quartz, do not show hexagonal (hexad) symmetry but have

Table 1. *The seven crystal systems, their corresponding Bravais lattices and symmetries*

System	Bravais lattices	Axial lengths and angles	Characteristic (minimum) symmetry	Point groups	
				Enantiomorphous	Non-enantiomorphous
Cubic	P I F	$a=b=c$ $\alpha=\beta=\gamma=90°$	4 triads equally inclined at 109.47°	23, 432	*m3, $\bar{4}$3m, *m3m
Tetragonal	P I	$a=b\neq c$ $\alpha=\beta=\gamma=90°$	1 rotation tetrad or inversion tetrad	4, 42	$\bar{4}$, *4/m, *4/mmm 4mm, $\bar{4}$2m
Orthorhombic	P I C F	$a\neq b\neq c$ $\alpha=\beta=\gamma=90°$	3 diads equally inclined at 90°	222	2mm, *mmm
Trigonal	$\begin{bmatrix}P\end{bmatrix}$ R	$a=b=c$ $\alpha=\beta=\gamma\neq90°$	1 rotation triad or inversion triad (= triad + centre of symmetry)	3, 32	*$\bar{3}$, 3m, *$\bar{3}$m
Hexagonal	$\begin{bmatrix}P\end{bmatrix}$	$a=b\neq c$ $\alpha=\beta=90°$, $\gamma=120°$	1 rotation hexad or inversion hexad (= triad + perp. mirror plane)	6, 62	$\bar{6}$, *6/m, *6/mmm 6mm, $\bar{6}$2m
Monoclinic	P C	$a\neq b\neq c$ $\alpha=\gamma=90°\neq\beta>90°$	1 rotation diad or inversion diad (= mirror plane)	2	m, *2/m
Triclinic	P	$a\neq b\neq c$ $\alpha\neq\beta\neq\gamma\neq90°$	None	1	*$\bar{1}$

*Centred point group.

triad symmetry. Such crystals are assigned to the **trigonal system** rather than to the hexagonal system. Hence the trigonal system includes crystals with both hexagonal and rhombohedral Bravais lattices. There is yet another problem which is particularly associated with the trigonal system, which is that the rhombohedral unit cell outlined in Figures 3.1 and 3.3 is not always used—a larger (non-primitive) unit cell of three times the size is sometimes more convenient. The problem of transforming axes from one unit cell to another is addressed in Chapter 5.

The crystal systems and their corresponding Bravais lattices are shown in Table 1. Notice that there are no axes or planes of symmetry in the **triclinic system**. The only symmetry that the triclinic lattice possesses (and which is possessed by all the other lattices) is a **centre of symmetry**. This point symmetry element, and also inversion axes of symmetry, are explained in Chapter 4.

Exercises

1. The drawings in Figure 3.6 show patterns of points distributed in orthorhombic-shaped unit cells. Identify to which (if any) of the orthorhombic Bravais lattices, *P*, *C*, *I* or *F*, each pattern of points corresponds.

   (*Hint:* It is helpful to sketch plans of several unit cells, which will show more clearly the patterns of points, and then to outline (if possible) a *P*, *C*, *I* or *F* unit cell.)

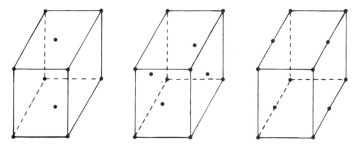

Fig. 3.6. Patterns of points in orthorhombic unit cells.

2. The unit cells of several **orthorhombic** structures are described below. Draw *plans* of each and identify the Bravais lattice, *P*, *C*, *I* or *F*, in each case.
   (a) One atom per unit cell located at $(x'y'z')$.
   (b) Two atoms per unit cell of the *same* type located at $(0\frac{1}{2}0)$ and $(\frac{1}{2}0\frac{1}{2})$.
   (c) Two atoms per unit cell, one type located at $(00z')$ and $(\frac{1}{2}\frac{1}{2}z')$ and the other type at $(00(\frac{1}{2}+z'))$ and $(\frac{1}{2}\frac{1}{2}(\frac{1}{2}+z'))$.

   (*Hint:* Draw plans of several unit cells and relocate the origin of the axes. x', y', z' should be taken as small (non-integral) fractions of the cell edge lengths.)

4 Crystal symmetry, point groups and crystal structures: the external symmetry of crystals

4.1 Symmetry and crystal habit

As indicated in Chapter 3, the system to which a crystal belongs may be identified from its observed or external symmetry. Sometimes this is a very simple procedure. For example, crystals which are found to grow or form as cubes obviously belong to the cubic system: the external point symmetry of the crystal and that of the underlying unit cell are identical. However, a crystal from the cubic system may not grow or form with the external shape of a cube; the unit cells may stack up to form, say, an octahedron, or a tetrahedron as shown in the models constructed from sugar cube unit cells (Fig. 4.1). These are just two examples of a very general phenomenon throughout all the crystal systems: only very occasionally do crystals grow with the same shape as that of the underlying unit cell. The different shapes or **habits** adopted by crystals are determined by chemical and physical factors which do not, at the moment, concern us; what does concern us as crystallographers is to know how to recognize to which system a crystal belongs even though its habit may be quite different from, and therefore conceal, the shape of the underlying unit cell.

Fig. 4.1. Stacking of 'sugar-cube' unit cells to form (a) a cube, (b) an octahedron and (c) a tetrahedron. Note that the cubic unit cells in all three models are in the same orientation.

The clue to the answer lies in the point group symmetry of the crystal. Consider, for example, the symmetry of the cubic crystals which have the shape or habit of a cube, an octahedron or a tetrahedron (Figs 4.1 and 4.2) or construct models of them (Appendix 1). The cube and octahedron, although they are different shapes, possess the same point group symmetry. The tetrahedron, however, has less symmetry: only six mirror planes instead of nine: only three diads running between opposite edges (i.e. along the directions perpendicular to the cube faces in the underlying cubes) and, as before, four triads running through each corner. The common, unchanged symmetry elements are the four (equally inclined) triads, and it is the presence of these triads which characterizes crystals belonging to the cubic system. Cubic crystals usually possess additional symmetry elements—the most symmetrical cubic crystals being those with the full point group symmetry of the underlying unit cell. But it is the four triads—not the three tetrads or the nine mirror planes—which are the 'hallmark' of a cubic crystal.

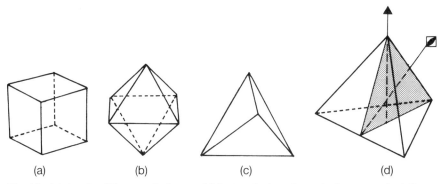

| (a) | (b) | (c) | (d) |

Fig. 4.2. (a) A cube, (b) an octahedron and (c) a tetrahedron drawn in the same orientation as the models in Figure 4.1. (d) A tetrahedron showing the positions of one variant of the point symmetry elements (mirror plane (shaded) ($\times 6$), triad ($\times 4$) and inversion tetrad (which includes a diad) ($\times 3$)).

Similar considerations apply to all the other crystal systems. For example, Figure 4.3 shows three orthorhombic crystals. Figure 4.3(a) shows a crystal with the full symmetry of the underlying unit cell—three perpendicular mirror planes and three perpendicular diads; Figure 4.3(b) shows a crystal will only two mirror planes and one diad along their line of intersection. Figure 4.3(c) shows a crystal with three perpendicular diads but no mirror planes.

4.2 The thirty-two crystal classes

The examples shown in Figures 4.1–4.3 are of crystals with different point group symmetries: they are said to belong to different **crystal classes**. Crystals in the same class have the same point group symmetry, so in effect the terms are synonymous. Notice that crystals in the same class do not

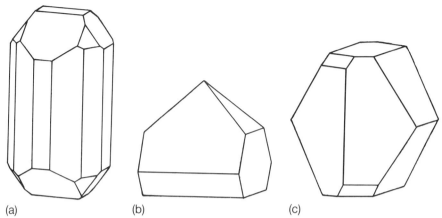

Fig. 4.3. Orthorhombic crystals (a) PbSO$_4$ (*mmm*), (b) NH$_4$MgPO$_4$·6H$_2$O (*2mm*), (c) MgSO$_4$·7H$_2$O (222) (from *Introduction to Crystallography* (3rd edn), by F. C. Phillips, Longman, 1977).

necessarily have the same shape. For example, the cube and the octahedron are obviously different shapes but belong to the same class because their point group symmetry is the same.

In two dimensions (Chapter 2) we found that there were ten plane point groups; in three dimensions there are thirty-two three-dimensional point groups. One of the great achievements of the science of mineralogy in the nineteenth century was the systematic description of the thirty-two point groups or crystal classes and their division into the seven crystal systems. Particular credit is due to J. F. C. Hessel*, whose contributions to the understanding of point group symmetry were unrecognized until after his death. The concept of seven different types or shapes of underlying unit cells then links up with the concept of the fourteen Bravais lattices; in other words, it establishes the connection between the external crystalline form or shape and the internal molecular or atomic arrangements.

It is not necessary to describe all the thirty-two point groups systematically; only the nomenclature for describing their important distinguishing features needs to be considered. This requires a knowledge of additional symmetry elements—centres and inversion axes.

4.3 Centres and Inversion axes of symmetry

If a crystal, or indeed any object, possesses a **centre of symmetry**, then any line passing through the centre of the crystal connects equivalent faces, or atoms, or molecules. A familiar example is a right hand and a left hand placed palm-to-palm but with the fingers pointing in opposite directions, as in Figure 4.4(a). Lines joining thumb to thumb or fingertip to fingertip all pass through a centre of symmetry between the hands. When the hands are placed

*Denotes biographical notes available in Appendix 3.

Fig. 4.4. Right and left hands (a) disposed with a centre of symmetry between them and (b) disposed with a mirror plane between them.

palm-to-palm but with the fingers pointing in the same direction, as in prayer, then there is no centre of symmetry but a mirror plane of symmetry instead, as in Figure 4.4(b). In two dimensions a centre of symmetry is equivalent to diad symmetry. [See, for example, the motif and plane molecule shown in Figure 2.3(c), which may be described as showing diad symmetry or a centre of symmetry.] In three dimensions this is not the case, as an inspection of Figure 4.4(a) will show.

Inversion axes of symmetry are rather difficult to describe (and therefore difficult for the reader to understand) without the use of the stereographic projection. This is a method of representing a three-dimensional pattern of planes in a crystal on a two-dimensional plan. Geographers have the same problem when trying to represent the surface of the Earth on a two-dimensional map, and they too make use of the stereographic projection. In atlases, the circular maps of the world (usually with the North or South Poles in the centre) are often stereographic projections.

Inversion axes are *compound* symmetry elements, consisting of a rotation followed by an inversion. For example, as described in (Chapter 2), the operation of a tetrad (four-fold) rotation axis is to repeat a crystal face or pattern every 90° rotation, e.g. the four repeating **R**s (Fig. 2.3) or the four-fold pattern of faces in a cube [Fig. 3.5(a)]. The operation of an inversion tetrad, symbol ▰ or $\overline{4}$ is to repeat a crystal face or pattern every 90° rotation-plus-inversion through a centre. What results is a four-fold pattern of faces around the inversion axis, but with each alternate face inverted. Examples of a crystal and an object with inversion tetrad axes are shown in Figures 4.5(a) and (b). The tennis ball has, in fact, the same point group symmetry as the crystal. Notice that when it is rotated 90° about the axis indicated, the 'downwards' loop in the surface pattern is replaced by an 'upwards' loop. Another 90° rotation brings a 'downwards' loop and so on for the full 360° rotation. Notice also that the inversion tetrad includes a diad, as is indicated by the diad (lens) symbol in the inversion tetrad (open square) symbol, ▰ or $\overline{4}$.

Finally, compare the symmetry of the tetragonal crystal in Figure 4.5(a)

(a)

(b)

Fig. 4.5. Examples of a crystal and an object which have inversion tetrad axes (both point group $\overline{4}2m$). (a) Urea $CO(NH_2)_2$ and (b) a tennis ball.

with that of the tetrahedron [Fig. 4.2(d)]: the diad axes which we recognized passing through the centres of opposite edges in the tetrahedron are, in fact, inversion tetrad axes or, to develop one of the points made in Section 4.1, stacking the cubes into the form of a tetrahedron reduces the symmetry element along the cube axis directions from rotation to inversion tetrad.

There are also inversion axes corresponding to rotation diads, triads and hexads. The operation of an inversion hexad, for example, is a rotation of 60° plus an inversion, this compound operation being repeated a total of six times until we return to the beginning. However, for a beginner to the subject, these axes may perhaps be regarded as being of lesser importance than inversion tetrads because they can be represented by combinations of other (better-understood) symmetry elements. The inversion diad is equivalent to a perpendicular mirror plane. The inversion triad is equivalent to a rotation triad plus a centre of symmetry—which is the symmetry of a rhombohedral lattice [see Fig. 3.1]. Notice that the 'top' three faces of the rhombohedron are related to the 'bottom' three faces by a centre of symmetry. An inversion hexad is equivalent to a triad with a perpendicular mirror plane. Again, these equivalences are best understood with the use of the stereographic projection. The important point is that only inversion tetrads are unique (i.e. they cannot be represented by a combination of rotation axes, centres or mirror planes) and therefore need to be considered separately.

The point group symmetries of the 32 classes are described by a 'shorthand' notation or **point group symbol** which lists the main (but not necessarily all) symmetry elements present. For example, the presence of centres of symmetry is not recorded because they may arise 'automatically' from the presence of other symmetry elements, e.g. the presence of an inversion triad mentioned above. This notation for the thirty-two crystal classes or point groups, and their distribution among the seven crystal systems, is fully worked out in the *International Tables for X-ray Crystallography* published for the International Union of Crystallography and in F. C. Phillips' *Introduction to Crystallography* (3rd edn) (Longman, 1977). Altogether there are five cubic classes, three orthorhombic classes, three monoclinic classes and so on. They are all listed in Table 1 (p. 39). The order in which the symmetry elements are written down in the point group symbol depends upon the crystal system. In the cubic system the first place in the symbol refers to the axes and/or planes of symmetry associated with the x-, y- or z-axes, the second refers to the four triads and the third to the axes and/or planes of symmetry associated with the face diagonal directions. Hence the point group symbol for the cube or the octahedron—the most symmetrical of the cubic crystals—is $4/m\ 3\ 2/m$. This full point group symbol is usually (and rather unhelpfully) contracted to $m3m$ because the operation of the four triads and nine mirror planes (three parallel to the cube faces and six parallel to the face diagonals) 'automatically' generates the three tetrads and six diads. The symbol for the tetrahedron is $\bar{4}3m$, the $\bar{4}$ referring to the three inversion tetrad axes along the x-, y- and z-axes and the m to the face-diagonal mirror planes. The least symmetrical cubic class has point group symbol 23, i.e. it only has diads along the x-, y- and z-axes and the characteristic four triads. The three places in the point group symbol in the orthorhombic system refer to the symmetry elements associated with the x-, y- and z-axes. The most symmetrical class [Fig. 4.3(a)], which has the full point group symmetry of the underlying orthorhombic unit cell (Fig. 3.5), has the full point group symbol $2/m$ $2/m$ $2/m$, but this is usually abbreviated to mmm because the presence of the three mirror planes perpendicular to the x-, y- and z-axes 'automatically' generates the three perpendicular diads. The other two classes are $2mm$ [Fig. 4.3(b)]—a diad along the intersection of two mirror planes—and 222 [Fig. 4.3(c)]—three perpendicular diads.

In the monoclinic system the point group symbol simply refers to the symmetry elements associated with the y-axis. This may be a diad (class 2); an inversion diad [equivalent to a perpendicular mirror plane (class $\bar{2}$ or m)] and a diad plus a perpendicular mirror plane (class $2/m$).

In the tetragonal, hexagonal and trigonal systems the first place in the point group symbol refers to the 'unique' z-axis. For example, the tetragonal crystals in Figure 4.5 have point group symmetry $\bar{4}2m$; $\bar{4}$ referring to the inversion tetrad along the z-axis, 2 referring to the diads along the x- and y-axes and m to the mirror planes which bisect the x- and y-axes (which you will find by examining the model!). One of the trigonal classes has point group symbol 32 (not to be confused with cubic class 23!), i.e. a single triad along the z-axis and (three) perpendicular diads.

Not all classes are of equal importance; in two of them (432 and $\bar{6} = 3/m$) there may be no examples of real crystals at all! On the other hand, the two monoclinic classes m and $2/m$ contain about 50 per cent of all crystalline materials on a 'crystal counting' basis, including feldspar, the commonest mineral in nature, and many other economically important minerals. The commonest class in any system is the **holosymmetric** class, i.e. the class which shows the highest symmetry. The holosymmetric cubic class $m3m$, the most symmetrical of all, contains only a few per cent of all crystals on this basis, but these also include many materials and ceramics of economic and commercial importance.

4.4 Crystal symmetry and properties

One major use of point groups is in relating crystal symmetry and properties, as the external symmetry of crystals arises from the symmetry of the internal atomic or molecular arrangements and these, in turn, determine or influence the crystal properties. Hence it is necessary to understand crystal symmetry to understand crystal properties. For example, the phenomena of pyro- and piezo-electricity—the separation of electric charge when a crystal is cooled/heated or stressed—can occur only in non-centrosymmetric crystals, of which there are twenty-one classes (Table 1). The phenomenon of optical activity or rotatory polarization can occur only in enantiomorphic crystals, i.e. those which have no mirror planes or inversion axes and which can therefore exist as 'right-' and 'left-'handed forms. A famous example is tartaric acid (Fig. 4.6). In 1848 Louis Pasteur* first noticed these two forms 'hemihedral to the right' and 'hemihedral to the left' under the microscope and, having separated them, found that their solutions were optically active in opposite senses.

Fig. 4.6. The 'right-handed' and 'left-handed' enantiomorphic forms of tartaric acid (from F. C. Phillips, *loc. cit.*).

4.5 Translational symmetry elements

The thirty-two point group symmetries (Table 1, page 39) may be applied to three-dimensional patterns just as the ten plane point group symmetries are applied to two-dimensional patterns (Chapter 2). As in two dimensions where translational symmetry elements or glide lines arise, so also in three dimensions do **glide planes** and also **screw axes** arise. It is only necessary to state the symmetry properties of patterns that are described by these translational symmetry elements. Glide planes are the three-dimensional analogues of glide lines; they define the symmetry in which mirror-related parts of the motif are shifted half a lattice spacing. In Figure 2.9 the figures are related by glide lines, which can easily be visualized as glide-plane symmetry. Glide planes are symbolized as *a*, *b*, *c* (according to whether the translation is along the *x*-, *y*- or *z*-axes), *n* or *d* (diagonal or diamond glide— special cases involving translations along more than one axis).

Screw axes (for which there is no two-dimensional analogue) essentially describe helical patterns of atoms or molecules, or the helical symmetry of motifs. Several types of helices are possible and they are all based upon different combinations of rotation axes and translations. Figure 4.7(a) shows one possible combination: a hexad axis coupled with a translation of half a lattice spacing for each 60° rotation. This screw hexad gives a helix with a pitch of three lattice spacings which is repeated every six atoms. It is represented by the symbol 6_3 (or in diagrams by the symbol ◕) the 6 referring to the 60° hexad rotation and the subscript 3 referring to the pitch of the helix. This particular screw hexad occurs in the hcp structure [as

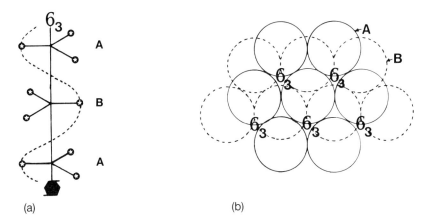

Fig. 4.7. (a) A screw hexad (6_3) axis, (b) location of these 6_3 axes in the hcp structure.

shown in Figure 4.7(b)]. Notice that the axes run parallel to the c-axis and are located in the 'unfilled' channels which occur in the hcp structure (labelled C in Fig. 1.4). They do not pass through the atom centres of either the A layer or B layer atoms; these are the positions of the triad axes (not hexad axes) in the hcp structure.

Just as the external symmetry of crystals does not distinguish between primitive and centred Bravais lattices, so also does it not distinguish between glide and mirror planes, or screw and rotation axes. For example, the six faces of an hcp crystal show hexad, six-fold symmetry, whereas the under-lying structure possesses only screw hexad, 6_3 symmetry.

4.6 Space groups

In Section 2.4 it was shown how the seventeen possible two-dimensional patterns or plane groups (Fig. 2.6) can be described as a combination of the five plane lattices with the appropriate point and translational symmetry elements. Similarly, in three dimensions, it can be shown that there are 230 possible three-dimensional patterns or **space groups**, which arise when the fourteen Bravais lattices are combined with the appropriate point and trans-lational symmetry elements. It is easy to see why there should be a sub-stantially larger number of space groups than plane groups. There are fourteen space lattices compared with only five plane lattices, but more particularly there is a greater number of combinations of point and trans-lational symmetry elements in three dimensions, particularly the presence of inversion axes (point) and screw axes (translational) which do not occur in two-dimensional patterns.

The first step in the derivation of the 230 space groups was made by L. Sohncke* (who also first introduced the notion of screw axes and glide planes described in Section 4.5). Essentially, Sohncke relaxed the restriction in the definition of a Bravais lattice—that the environment of each point is identical—by considering the possible arrays of points which have identical environments when viewed from *different* directions, rather than from the *same* direction as in the definition of a Bravais lattice. This is equivalent to combining the fourteen Bravais lattices with the appropriate translational symmetry elements, and gives rise to a total of sixty-five space groups or Sohncke groups.

The second, final step was to account for inversion axes of symmetry which gives rise to a further 165 space groups. They were first worked out by Fedorov in Moscow in 1890 (who drew heavily on Sohncke's work) and independently by Schoenflies in Göttingen in 1891 and Barlow* in London in 1894—an example of the frequently occurring phenomenon in science of progress being made almost at the same time by people approaching a problem entirely independently. The 230 space groups are systematically described in the *International Tables for Crystallography*. The convention now most generally adopted is that due to Hermann* and Mauguin*. However, not all the 230 Hermann–Mauguin space group symbols will be described; only their most salient characteristics will be covered together with one example.

The space group symbol consists first of a letter *P*, *C*, *I*, *F* or *R*, which describes the Bravais lattice type; then a statement, rather like a point group symbol, of the essential (not all) symmetry elements present. For example, the space group symbol *Pba2* represents a space group which has a primitive (*P*) Bravais lattice and whose point group is *mm2* (the *a* and *b* glide planes being simple mirror planes in point group symmetry. This is one of the point groups of the orthorhombic system [Fig. 4.3(b)] and the lattice type is orthorhombic *P*.

The space group itself is represented by means of two diagrams, usually plotted as projections or plans in the *x–y* plane (i.e. the *z*-axis is out of the plane of the paper). One of these plans shows the positions of all the symmetry elements present. The other shows the operation of these symmetry elements on an asymmetrical 'unit of pattern' represented as the symbol ○ (i.e. corresponding to the **R** in our two-dimensional case), as shown in Figure 2.1. In other words, the symbol ○ may represent an asymmetric molecule, a group of molecules or, indeed, any asymmetrical structural unit. It is placed at small fractions of the cell edge lengths x' y' z' away from the origin of the lattice, the z' parameter being represented by a plus sign in a projection along the *z*-axis (see Exercise 2, Chapter 3); this is called a 'general position' because it does not lie on a non-translational symmetry element, i.e. at a centre of symmetry, on a mirror plane, or on an axis (rotational or inversion) of symmetry. The resulting set of atomic positions is known as the 'general equivalent positions'.

Figure 4.8 gives the two diagrams for space group *Pba2*. In Figure 4.8(b) the diad axes are shown parallel to the *z*-axis and passing through every corner of the cell (i.e. through rows of lattice points), and the *a* and *b* glide planes are shown by dashed lines. Again, they run parallel to the *z*-axis but lie between the diad axes. The operation of these symmetry elements on the pattern unit ○ is shown in Figure 4.8(a); the operation of the diads is to repeat the ○ after 180° rotation in exactly the same way as in the two-dimensional case (see Fig. 2.3). The operation of the glide planes is to reflect the ○ to give its mirror image, which is represented by the symbol ①, i.e. corresponding to the Я in our two-dimensional case (Fig. 2.1), and then to translate it half a lattice spacing along the *y*- or *x*-axis. Hence we arrive at the pattern of right- and left-handed asymmetrical units, ○ and ①, shown in Figure 4.8(a) which is the space group *Pba*2. Notice that the operation of the diads through the corners of the unit cell 'automatically' generates additional diads in between. *All* the symmetry elements which arise in the space group are shown in Figure 4.8(b). Notice too that if the pattern-unit ○ were to be placed not in a general position but in a 'special position', on a diad axis in this example, then a simpler pattern, with fewer general equivalent positions, results.

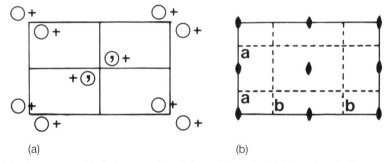

(a)   (b)

Fig. 4.8. Space group *Pba*2 shown projected down the *z*-axis. (a) General equivalent positions within the unit cell and (b) positions of the symmetry elements.

All the other 229 space groups can be built up in the same way, although it will be clear that the more symmetrical the crystal, and the greater the number and types of symmetry elements present, the more complicated the pattern will be. Cubic space groups are therefore the most 'complicated', as a glance at the International Tables will show. However, remember that these complicated patterns of structural or pattern units do not mean that cubic crystals have necessarily more complicated structures. The space groups as drawn represent the most general case. As we saw above for space group *Pba*2, when the pattern unit, the ○, is placed on a diad axis of symmetry, i.e. a 'special position', a simpler pattern results. So also when the atoms are in special positions in the higher-symmetry crystals, and the greater the number of symmetry elements, the greater the simplification.

4.7 Bravais lattices, motifs and crystal structures

In the simple cubic, bcc and ccp structures of the elements, the three cubic lattices (Fig. 3.1) have exactly the same arrangement of lattice points as the atoms, i.e. in these examples the motif is just one atom. In more complex crystals the motif consists of more than one atom and, to determine the Bravais lattice of a crystal, it is necessary first to identify the motif and then to identify the arrangement of the motifs. In crystals consisting of two or more different types of atoms this procedure may be quite difficult, but fortunately simple examples best illustrate the procedure and the principles involved. For example, in NaCl [isomorphous with TiN; see Figure 1.14(a)], the motif is one sodium and one chlorine ion and the motifs are arranged in an fcc array. Hence the Bravais lattice of NaCl and TiN is cubic *F*.

In Li_2O [isomorphous with TiH_2; see Figure 1.14(b)] the motif is one oxygen and two lithium atoms; the motifs are arranged in an fcc array and the Bravais lattice of these compounds is cubic *F*. In ZnS [isomorphous with TiH; see Figure 1.14(c)] the motif is one zinc and one sulphur atom; again, these are arranged in an fcc array and the Bravais lattice of these compounds is cubic *F*. All the crystal structures illustrated in Figure 1.14 have the cubic *F* Bravais lattice. They are called face-centred cubic structures not because the arrangements of atoms are the same—clearly they are not—but because they all have the cubic *F* lattice.

In CsCl [Fig. 1.12(b)], the motif is one caesium and one chlorine ion; the motifs are arranged in a simple cubic array and the Bravais lattice is cubic *P*. To be sure, the arrangement of ions in CsCl (and compounds isomorphous with it) is such that there is an ion or atom at the body-centre of the unit cell, but the Bravais lattice is *not* cubic *I* because the ions or atoms at the corners and centre of the unit cell are different. Nor, for the same reason, should CsCl and compounds isomorphous with it be described as having a body-centred cubic structure.

In the case of hexagonal structures the arrangement of lattice points in the hexagonal *P* lattice (Fig. 3.1) corresponds to the arrangement of atoms in the simple hexagonal structure [Fig. 1.5(a)] and *not* the hcp structure [Fig. 1.5(b)]. In the simple hexagonal structure the environment of all the atoms is identical and the motif is just one atom. In the hcp structure the environment of the atoms in the A and B layers is different. The motif is a pair of atoms, i.e. an A layer and a B layer atom per lattice point. The environment of these pairs of atoms (as for the pairs of ions or atoms in the NaCl, or CsCl or ZnS structures) is identical and they are arranged on a simple hexagonal lattice.

Exercises

1. Draw the space group *Pba*2 with the pattern unit $\bigcirc$ at the following positions:
   (a) on the *b* glide plane, i.e. at $(x' \frac{1}{4} z')$;

(b) at the intersections of the *a* and *b* glide planes, i.e. at $(\frac{1}{4}\frac{1}{4}z')$;

(c) on a diad axis through the origin, i.e. at $(00z')$;

(d) on a diad axis through the mid-points of the cell edges, i.e. at $(\frac{1}{2}0z')$.

Hence, show that only (c) and (d) constitute special positions.

2. Make and examine the crystal models of NaCl, CsCl, diamond, ZnS (sphalerite), ZnS (wurtzite), Li_2O or CaF_2 (fluorite), $CaTiO_3$ (perovskite). Identify the Bravais lattice and describe the motif of each structure.

5 Describing lattice planes and directions in crystals: Miller indices and zone axis symbols

5.1 Introduction

In previous chapters we have described the distributions of atoms in crystals, the symmetry of crystals and the concept of Bravais lattices and unit cells. We now introduce what are essentially shorthand notations for describing directions and planes in crystals (whether or not they correspond to axes or planes of symmetry). The great advantages of these notations are that they are short, unambiguous and easily understood. For example, the direction (or zone axis) symbol for the 'corner-to-corner' (or triad axis) directions in a cube is simply ⟨111⟩. The plane index (or Miller index) for the faces of a cube is simply {100} or of an octahedron, {111} (Fig. 4.1). The various faces and the directions of their intersections in crystals such as those illustrated in Figure 4.3 can also be precisely described using these notations. Without them one would have to resort to carefully scaled drawings or projections.

Now direction symbols and plane indices are based upon the crystal axes or lattice vectors which outline or define the unit cell (see Section 3.2) and the only ambiguities which can arise occur in those cases in which different unit cells may be used. For example, crystals with the cubic F Bravais lattice may be described in terms of the 'conventional' face-centred cell (Fig. 1.6) or in terms of the primitive rhombohedral cell (Fig. 1.7). Because the axes are different, the direction symbols and plane indices will also be different. Hence it is important to know (1) which set of crystal axes, or which unit cell, is being used and (2) how to change or transform direction symbols and plane indices when the set of crystal axes or the unit cell is changed. This topic is covered in Section 5.8. It is a serious problem only in the case of the trigonal system for crystals with a rhombohedral lattice where there are two almost equally 'popular' unit cells—unlike, say, the rhombohedral cells for the cubic F and cubic I lattices which are rarely used. In addition, in the trigonal and hexagonal systems it is possible to introduce, because of symmetry considerations, a fourth axis, giving rise to 'Miller–Bravais' plane indices and 'Weber' direction symbols, each of which consist of four, rather than three, numbers. This topic is covered in Section 5.7, but first the concept of a zone and zone axis needs to be explained, a topic which is covered in more detail in Section 5.6.

A **zone** may be defined as 'a set of faces or planes in a crystal whose intersections are all parallel'. The common direction of the intersections is called the **zone axis**. All directions in crystals are zone axes, so the terms 'direction' and 'zone axis' are synonymous. So much for the definition. The concept of a zone is readily understood by examining an ordinary pencil. The six faces of a pencil all form or lie in a zone because they all intersect along one direction—the pencil lead direction—which is the zone axis for this set of faces. The number of faces in a zone is not restricted and the faces need not be crystallographically equivalent. For example, the edges of a pencil may be shaved flat to give a 12-sided pencil, i.e. an additional six faces in the zone. Or consider an orthorhombic crystal [Fig. 3.5(b)], or a matchbox. Each crystal axis is the zone axis for four faces, or two crystallographically equivalent pairs of faces. Each face lies in two zones; for example, the 'top' and 'bottom' faces of Figure 3.5(b) lie in the zones which have the *x*- and *y*-directions as zone axes. In general, a face or plane in a crystal belongs to a whole 'family' of zones, the zone axes of which must lie in or be parallel to the face.

Verbal definitions are frequently rather clumsy in relation to the simple concepts which they seek to express. Take a piece of paper and draw on it some parallel lines. Fold the paper along the lines—and there you have a zone.

5.2 Indexing lattice directions—zone axis symbols

First, the direction whose symbol is to be determined must pass through the origin of the unit cell. Consider the unit cell shown in Figure 5.1, which has unit cell edge vectors **a, b, c** (which are not necessarily orthogonal or equal in length). The steps for determining the zone axis symbol for the direction 0L are as follows. Write down the co-ordinates of a point—any point—in this

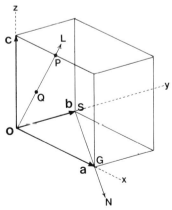

Fig. 5.1. Primitive unit cell of a lattice defined by unit cell vectors **a, b, c**. OL and SN are directions [102] and [1̄10] respectively.

direction—say P—in terms of fractions of the lengths *a, b* and *c* respectively. The co-ordinates of P are $\frac{1}{2}$, 0, 1. Now express these fractions as the ratio of whole numbers and insert them into [square] brackets without commas; hence [102]. This is then the direction or zone axis symbol for 0L. Notice that if we had chosen a different point along 0L—say Q—with co-ordinates $\frac{1}{4}$, 0, $\frac{1}{2}$, we should have obtained the same result.

Now consider the direction SN. To find its direction symbol the origin must be shifted from 0 to S. Proceeding as before (e.g. finding the co-ordinates of G with respect to the origin at S) gives the direction symbol [1$\bar{1}$0] (pronounced one bar-one oh), the bar or minus sign referring to a co-ordinate in the negative sense along the crystal axis.

Directions in crystals are, of course, vectors, which may be expressed in terms of components on the three unit cell edge or 'base' vectors **a, b** and **c**. In the above example the direction 0L is written

$$\mathbf{r}_{102} = 1\mathbf{a} + 0\mathbf{b} + 2\mathbf{c}.$$

The general symbol for a direction is [*uvw*] or, written as a vector:

$$\mathbf{r}_{uvw} = u\mathbf{a} + v\mathbf{b} + w\mathbf{c}.$$

The direction symbols for the unit cell edge vectors **a, b** and **c** are [100], [010] and [001], and very often these symbols are used in preference to the terms *x*-axis, *y*-axis and *z*-axis.

5.3 Indexing lattice planes—Miller indices

First, for reasons which will be apparent shortly, the lattice plane whose index is to be determined must not pass through the origin of the unit cell, or rather the origin must be shifted to a corner of the cell which does not lie in the plane. Consider the unit cell in Figure 5.2 (identical to Figure 5.1 but drawn separately to avoid confusion). We shall determine the index of the lattice plane which is shaded and outlined by the letters RMS. It is important first to realize that this plane extends indefinitely through the crystal; the shaded area is simply that portion of the plane that lies within the unit cell of Figure 5.2. It is also important to realize that we are not just considering *one* plane but a whole *family* of identical, parallel planes passing through the crystal. The next plane 'up' in the family is also shaded within the confines of the unit cell and is outlined by the letters PGFH. There is a whole succession of such planes, including one which passes through the origin of the unit cell.

A two-dimensional sketch (Fig. 5.3) of Figure 5.2, with the *x*- and *z*-axes in the plane of the paper, and showing the traces of these planes extending into neighbouring cells, will make this clear. Figure 5.3 also shows that all the planes in the family are identical in that they contain the same number or sequence of lattice points.

For RMS, the plane in the family nearest the origin, write down the

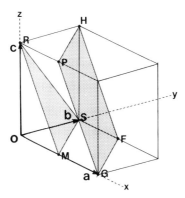

Fig. 5.2. Primitive unit cell (identical to Figure 5.1), showing the first two planes, RMS and PGFH, in the family. These planes are shaded within the confines of the unit cell.

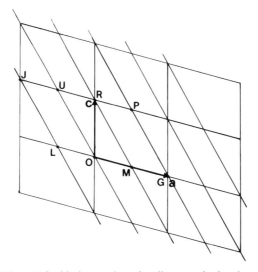

Fig. 5.3. Sketch of Figure 5.2 with the **a** and **c** unit cell vectors in the plane of the paper (**b** into the plane of the paper) showing traces JL, UO, RM, PG of a family of planes.

intercepts of the plane on the axes or unit cell vectors **a**, **b**, **c** respectively; they are $\frac{1}{2}a$, $1b$, $1c$. Expressed as fractions of the cell edge lengths we have $\frac{1}{2}$, 1, 1. Now take the *reciprocals* of these fractions, and put the whole numbers into (round) brackets without commas; hence (2 1 1). This is the **Miller index** of the plane, so-called after the crystallographer, W. H. Miller*, who first devised the notation. Proceeding similarly for the next plane in the family, PGFH (and considering its extension beyond the confines of the unit cell), we have intercepts $1a$, $2b$, $2c$, which expressed as fractions becomes 1, 2, 2;

*Denotes biographical notes available in Appendix 3.

the reciprocals of which are $1, \frac{1}{2}, \frac{1}{2}$, which expressed as whole numbers again gives the Miller index (2 1 1). The plane through the origin, 0U (Fig. 5.3), has intercepts 0, 0, 0 which gives an indeterminate 'Miller index' ($\infty\ \infty\ \infty$), but this is merely expressive of the fact that another corner of the unit cell must be selected as the origin. The plane JL (Fig. 5.3) in the same family lies on the opposite side of the origin from RM and has intercepts $-\frac{1}{2}a$, $-1b$, $-1c$ which gives the Miller index ($\bar{2}\ \bar{1}\ \bar{1}$) (pronounced bar-two, bar-one, bar-one), the bar signs simply being expressive of the fact that the planes are recorded from the opposite (negative axis) side of the origin.

The general index for a lattice plane is (hkl), i.e. (working backwards), the first plane in the family from the origin makes intercepts a/h, b/k, c/l on the axes. This provides us with an alternative method for determining the Miller index of a family of planes. Count the number of planes intercepted in passing from one corner of the unit cell to the next. For the family of planes (hkl) the first plane intercepts the x-axis at a distance a/h, the second at $2a/h$, and so on; i.e. a total of h planes are intercepted in passing from one corner of the unit cell to the next along the x-axis. Similarly, k planes are intercepted along the y-axis and l planes along the z-axis.

Miller indices apply not only to lattice planes, as sketched in Figures 5.2 and 5.3, but also to the external faces of crystals, where the origin is conventionally taken to be at the centre of the crystal. The intercepts of a crystal face will be many millions of lattice spacings from the origin, depending of course on the size of the crystal but the *ratios* of the fractional intercepts, and therefore the Miller indices, will be simple whole numbers as before. This is sometimes expressed as 'The Law of Rational Indices', the germ of which can be traced back to Haüy—see, for example, his representation of the relationship between the crystal faces and the unit cell in dog-tooth spar (Fig. 1.2).

When a crystal plane lies parallel to an axis its intercept on that axis is infinity, the reciprocal of which is zero. For example, the 'front' face of a crystal, i.e. the face which intersects the x-axis only and is parallel to the y- and z-axes, has Miller index (100); the 'top' face, which intersects the z-axis is (001) and so on. It is useful to remember that a zero Miller index means that the plane (or face) is parallel to the corresponding unit cell axis.

Although Miller indices never include fractions they may, when used to describe lattice planes, have common denominators and this occurs when the unit cell is non-primitive. Consider, for example, the lattice planes perpendicular to the x-axis in the cubic F unit cell (Fig. 5.4). Because of the presence of the face-centring lattice points, lattice planes are intersected every $\frac{1}{2}a$ distance along the x-axis. The first lattice plane in the family, shown shaded in Figure 5.4, makes fractional intercepts $\frac{1}{2}, \infty, \infty$ on the x-, y- and z-axes. The Miller index of this family of planes is therefore (200). To refer to them as (100) would be to ignore the 'interleaving' lattice planes within the unit cell. This distinction does not apply to the Miller indices of the external crystal faces, which are many millions of lattice planes from the origin.

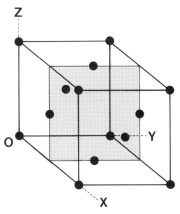

Fig. 5.4. A cubic *F* unit cell showing (shaded) the first plane from the origin of a family of planes perpendicular to the *x*-axis but with interplanar spacing *a*/2.

The procedure described above for defining plane indices may seem rather odd—why not simply express indices as fractional intercepts without taking reciprocals? The Law of Rational Indices gives half a clue, but the full significance can only be appreciated in terms of the reciprocal lattice (Chapter 6).

5.4 Miller indices and zone axis symbols in cubic crystals

Miller indices and zone axis symbols may be used to express the symmetry of crystals. This applies to crystals in all the seven systems, but the principles are best explained in relation to cubic crystals because of their high symmetry.

The positive and negative directions of the crystal axes *x*, *y*, *z* can be expressed by the direction symbols (Section 5.2) as [100], [$\bar{1}$00], [010], [0$\bar{1}$0], [001], [00$\bar{1}$]. Because, in the cubic system, the axes are crystallographically equivalent and interchangeable, so also are all these six direction symbols. They may be expressed collectively as ⟨100⟩, the ⟨triangular⟩ brackets implying all six permutations or variants of 1, 0, 0. Similarly, the triad axis corner-to-corner directions are expressed as ⟨111⟩, of which there are eight or four pairs of variants, namely, [11$\bar{1}$], [1$\bar{1}$$\bar{1}$]; [1$\bar{1}$1], [$\bar{1}1\bar{1}$]; [111], [$\bar{1}$$\bar{1}$1]; [111], [$\bar{1}$$\bar{1}$$\bar{1}$]. The diad axis (edge-to-edge) directions are ⟨110⟩, of which there are twelve or six pairs of variants. For the general direction ⟨*uvw*⟩ there are forty-eight or twenty-four pairs of variants.

A similar concept can be applied to Miller indices. The six faces of a cube (with the origin at the centre) are (100), ($\bar{1}$00), (010), (0$\bar{1}$0), (001), (00$\bar{1}$). These are expressed collectively as planes 'of the form' {100}, i.e. in {curly} brackets. Again, for the general plane {*hkl*} there are forty-eight or twenty-four pairs of variants.

In cubic crystals, directions are perpendicular to planes with the same numerical indices; for example, the direction [111] is perpendicular to the plane (111), or equivalently it is parallel to the normal to the plane (111). This parallelism between directions and normals to planes with the same numerical indices does not apply to crystals of lower symmetry except in special cases. This will be made clear by considering Figures 5.5(a) and (b), which show plans of unit cells perpendicular to the *z*-axis of a cubic and an orthorhombic crystal. The traces of the (110) planes and the [110] directions are shown in each case. Clearly, the (110) plane and [110] direction are only perpendicular to each other in the cubic crystal. In the orthorhombic crystal it is only in the special cases, e.g. (100) planes and [100] directions, that the directions are perpendicular to planes of the same numerical indices.

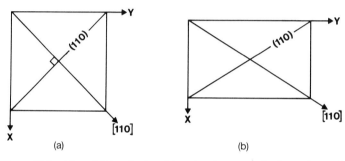

Fig. 5.5. Plans of (a) cubic and (b) orthorhombic unit cells perpendicular to the *z*-axis, showing the relationships between planes and zone axes of the same numerical indices.

5.5 Lattice plane spacings, Miller indices and Laue indices

The experimental technique which has been of the greatest importance in revealing the structure of crystals is undoubtedly X-ray diffraction.

The story of the discovery of X-ray diffraction in crystals by Laue*, Friedrich and Knipping in Munich in 1912 and the development of the technique by W. H. Bragg* and W. L. Bragg* in Leeds and Cambridge in the years preceding the First World War is well known. But why did the Braggs make such rapid advances in the analysis of X-ray diffraction photographs in comparison with Laue and his co-workers? An important factor in the answer seems to be that Laue envisaged crystals in terms of a three-dimensional network of rows of atoms and based his analysis on the notion that the crystal behaved, in effect, as a three-dimensional diffraction grating. This approach is not wrong, but it is in practice rather clumsy or protracted. On the other hand, the Braggs (and here the credit must go to W. L. Bragg, the son) envisaged crystals in terms of layers or planes of atoms which behaved in effect as reflecting planes (for which the angle of incidence equals the angle of reflection), strong 'reflected' beams being produced when the path differences between reflections from successive planes in a family equal to whole number of wavelengths. This approach is not correct in a physical sense—planes of atoms do not reflect X-rays as such—but it is correct in a geometrical sense and provides us with a beautifully simple expression, which every schoolchild knows, for the analysis of crystal structure:

$$n\lambda = 2d_{hkl}\sin\theta,$$

where λ is the wavelength, n is the order of reflection, d_{hkl} is the lattice plane spacing and θ is the angle of incidence/reflection to the planes.

What led W. L. Bragg to this novel perception of diffraction? Simply his observation of the elliptical shapes of the diffraction spots, which he noticed were also characteristic of the reflections from mirrors of a pencil-beam of light. Only connect!

The topics of X-ray and electron diffraction and the derivation of Bragg's Law are covered in Chapter 7. However, some of the geometrical properties of lattice planes now need to be considered.

The calculation for lattice plane spacings (also called interplanar spacings or d-spacings), d_{hkl}, is simple in the case of crystals with orthogonal axes. Consider Figure 5.6, which shows the first plane away from the origin in a family of (hkl) planes. As there is another plane in the family passing through the origin, the lattice plane spacing is simply the length of the normal 0N. Angle A0N $= \alpha$ (angle between normal and x-axis) and angle 0NA$= 90°$. Hence

$$0A \cos \alpha = 0N \quad \text{or} \quad (a/h) \cos \alpha = d \quad \text{or} \quad \cos \alpha = \frac{dh}{a}.$$

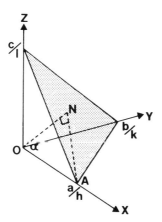

Fig. 5.6. Intercepts of a lattice plane (hkl) on the unit cell vectors **a, b, c**. ON$= d_{hkl} =$inter-planar spacing.

Given that β and γ (not shown in Figure 5.6) are the angles between 0N and the y- and z-axes respectively, then

$$\cos \beta = \frac{dk}{b} \quad \text{and} \quad \cos \gamma = \frac{dl}{c}.$$

For orthogonal axes $\cos^2\alpha + \cos^2\beta + \cos^2\gamma = 1$ (Pythagoras), hence

$$\left(\frac{dh}{a}\right)^2 + \left(\frac{dk}{b}\right)^2 + \left(\frac{dl}{c}\right)^2 = 1.$$

For a cubic crystal $a = b = c$, hence

$$\frac{1}{d^2} = \frac{h^2 + k^2 + l^2}{a^2}.$$

Except in the cases of non-primitive cells discussed above (Section 5.3) indices for lattice planes do not have common factors. However, the indices for reflecting planes frequently do have common factors. They are sometimes called **Laue indices** and are usually written without brackets. Their relationship with Miller indices for lattice planes is best illustrated by way of an example. Apply Bragg's Law to the (111) lattice planes in a crystal:

first-order reflection $(n = 1)$: $1\lambda = 2d_{111}\sin\theta_1$

second-order reflection $(n = 2)$: $2\lambda = 2d_{111}\sin\theta_2$, etc.

Now the order of reflection is written on the right-hand side, i.e. for the second-order reflection $(n = 2)$

$$1\lambda = 2\left(\frac{d_{111}}{2}\right)\sin\theta_2.$$

This suggests that second-order reflections from the (111) lattice planes of d-spacing d_{111} can be regarded as first-order reflections from planes of half the spacing, $d_{111}/2$. Halving the intercepts implies doubling the indices, so these planes are called 222 (no brackets) of d-spacing $d_{222} = d_{111}/2$. These 222 planes are imaginary in the sense that only half of them pass through lattice points, but they are a useful fiction in the sense that the order of reflection, n in Bragg's Law, can be omitted. Continuing the above example, third-order reflections from the (111) lattice planes can be regarded as first-order reflections from the 333 reflecting planes (only a third of which in a family pass through lattice points). As mentioned above, these unbracketed indices are sometimes called Laue indices or reflection indices.

However, it should be pointed out that, in practice, when analysing X-ray or electron diffraction patterns, crystallographers very often do not make this distinction between Miller indices and Laue indices, but simply refer, for example, to 333 reflections (no brackets) from (333) 'planes' (with brackets). This should not lead to any confusion, except perhaps in the case of centred lattices where lattice planes may have common factors. For example, the 200 reflecting planes in the cubic F lattice (Fig. 5.4) are also the (200) lattice planes, but the 200 reflecting planes in the cubic P lattice refer to second-order reflections from the (100) lattice planes.

5.6 Zones, zone axes and the zone law, the addition rule

The concept of a zone has been introduced in Section 5.1. In this section some useful geometrical relationships are listed, the proofs of which are given in Section 6.4, in which use is made of reciprocal lattice vectors. It is possible, of course, to prove the relationships given below without making use of the concept of the reciprocal lattice, but the proofs tend to be long, tedious and not very obvious.

5.6.1 The zone law (or Weiss* zone law)

If a plane (hkl) lies in a zone $[uvw]$ (i.e. if the direction $[uvw]$ is parallel to the plane (hkl)), then

$$hu + kv + lw = 0.$$

5.6.2 Zone axis at the intersection of two planes

The line or direction of intersection of two planes in a zone $(h_1k_1l_1)$ and $(h_2k_2l_2)$ gives the zone axis, $[uvw]$, where

$$u = (k_1l_2 - k_2l_1); \quad v = (l_1h_2 - l_2h_2); \quad w = (h_1k_2 - k_2h_1).$$

To remember these relationships, use the following 'memogram':

h_1	k_1	l_1	h_1	k_1	l_1
h_2	k_2	l_2	h_2	k_2	l_2
	u	v	w		

Write down the indices twice and strike out the first and last pairs. Then u is given by cross-multiplying, i.e.

$$u = (plus \; k_1l_2 \; minus \; k_2l_1),$$

and similarly for v and w.

5.6.3 Plane parallel to two directions

To find the plane lying parallel to two directions $[u,v,w]$ and $[u_2 v_2 w_2]$, write down the 'memogram'

$$
\begin{array}{c|cccc|c}
u_1 & v_1 & w_1 & u_1 & v_1 & w_2 \\
 & \diagdown\!\!\!\!\diagup_{+}^{-} & \diagdown\!\!\!\!\diagup_{+}^{-} & \diagdown\!\!\!\!\diagup_{+}^{-} & & \\
u_2 & v_2 & w_2 & u_2 & v_2 & w_2 \\
\hline
 & h & k & l &
\end{array}
$$

and proceed as above, i.e. $h = (v_1 w_2 - v_2 w_1)$, etc.

5.6.4 The addition rule

Consider two planes $(h_1 k_1 l_1)$ and $(h_2 k_2 l_2)$ lying in a zone. Then the index of another plane (HKL) in the zone lying between these planes is given by $H = (mh_1 + nh_2)$; $K = (mk_1 + nk_2)$; $L = (ml_1 + nl_2)$, where m and n are small whole numbers.

This rule enables us to work out the indices of 'in-between' planes in zones. Consider, for example, the plane marked P in Figure 5.7 which lies both in the zone containing (100) and (011) and the zone containing (101) and (110). We need to choose values of m and n such that adding the pairs of indices as above gives the same result of (HKL). This is much more easily done than said! The plane is (211), i.e.

$$(101) + (110) = (211) \qquad (m = 1, n = 1)$$
$$\text{and} \quad (011) + 2(100) = (211) \qquad (m = 1, n = 2).$$

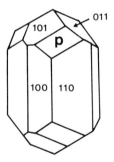

Fig. 5.7. A monoclinic crystal (class *m*) in which the face P lies in two zones, one containing (101) and (110), the other containing (011) and (100).

5.7 Indexing in the trigonal and hexagonal systems: Weber symbols and Miller–Bravais indices

As shown in Section 3.3, the rhombohedral and hexagonal lattices both consist of hexagonal layers of lattice points which in the rhombohedral lattice are 'stacked' in the ABCABC ... sequence [Fig. 3.3(b)] and in the hexagonal lattice are 'stacked' in the AAA ... sequence [Fig. 3.3(a)]. In both cases, it is convenient to outline unit cells using the easily recognized hexagonal layers as the 'base' of the cells and with the z-axis (or **c** vector) perpendicular thereto. However, at least three choices of unit cell are commonly made and these are illustrated in the case of the hexagonal lattice in Figure 5.8 (the corresponding unit cells of the rhombohedral lattice differ only insofar as they contain additional lattice points of the B and C layers at fractional distances of $\frac{1}{3}$ and $\frac{2}{3}$ of the unit cell edge length along the z-axis).

Figure 5.8(a) shows the primitive hexagonal unit cell, the smallest that can be chosen with the x- and y-axes at 120°. However, this is often inconvenient in that it does not reveal the hexagonal symmetry of the lattice. For example, all the (pencil) faces parallel to the z-axis are crystallographically equivalent or of the same form, but their indices differ in type as shown—some have indices of the type $(1\bar{1}0)$ and some have indices of the type (100). To overcome this problem a *fourth* axis—the u-axis—is inserted at 120° to both the x- and y-axes, as shown in Figure 5.8(b). These are called Miller–Bravais axes x, y, u, z (or vectors **a, b, t, c**) and the indices of the lattice planes, called Miller–Bravais indices, now consist of four numbers $(hkil)$. The indices for the pencil faces are shown in Figure 5.8(b) and they are all of the same form $\{10\bar{1}0\}$. Notice that, in all cases the sum of the first three numbers is zero, i.e. $h+k+i=0$. As therefore $i=-(h+k)$, it is sometimes simply represented as a dot, i.e. $\{hk.l\}$. However, this unnecessary abbreviation should be discouraged, as it defeats the object of using Miller–Bravais axes in the first place.

Similarly, zone axis symbols, sometimes called **Weber* symbols**, consist of four numbers $\langle UVTW \rangle$. However, determining these numbers (i.e. determining the components of a vector using four base vectors in three-dimensional space) is not straightforward. Essentially, the components of a vector are adjusted such that the sum of the first three numbers is zero, i.e. $U+V+T=0$. In practice, the simplest procedure is to determine first the

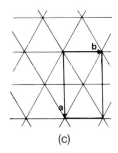

(a) (b) (c)

Fig. 5.8. Hexagonal net of the hexagonal P lattice showing (a) primitive hexagonal unit cell with the traces of the six prism faces indexed $\{hkl\}$, (b) hexagonal (four-index) unit cell with the traces of the six prism faces indexed $\{hkil\}$, (c) orthohexagonal (*Base* or *C*-centred) unit cell.

zone axis symbol [*uvw*] of a direction using three axes [Fig. 5.8(a)] and then transform these to [*UVTW*] using the following identities:

$$U = \tfrac{1}{3}(2u - v), \quad V = \tfrac{1}{3}(2v - u), \quad T = -(U + V), \quad W = w.$$

On this basis the zone axis symbols for the *x*-, *y*- and *u*-axes are [$2\bar{1}\bar{1}0$], [$\bar{1}2\bar{1}0$], [$\bar{1}\bar{1}20$] respectively. The reverse transformation from [*UVTW*] to [*uvw*] is given by the identities

$$u = (U - T), \quad v = (V - T), \quad w = W.$$

When using Miller–Bravais indices and Weber symbols, the zone law becomes

$$hU + kV + iT + lW = 0.$$

Another unit cell—the orthohexagonal cell—is shown in Figure 5.8(c). The ratio of the lengths of the edges, *a/b* is $\sqrt{3}$. As with the primitive hexagonal cell this does not reveal the hexagonal symmetry of the lattice. This base-centred cell has the advantage that the axes are orthogonal and is particularly useful in showing the relationships between crystals which have similar structures but where small distortions can change the symmetry from hexagonal to orthorhombic, i.e. in situations in which the ratio *a/b* is no longer precisely $\sqrt{3}$.

To summarize, great care must be taken in interpreting plane indices and zone-axis symbols in the hexagonal and trigonal systems—an index such as (111) could refer to the primitive hexagonal or orthohexagonal unit cell, or it could even refer to the Miller–Bravais hexagonal unit cell and be the contracted form of ($11\bar{2}1$), i.e. (11.1), in which the dot may have been omitted in printing!

5.8 Transforming Miller indices and zone axis symbols

As mentioned in Section 3.3, different choices of axes (i.e. different unit cells), are frequently encountered in trigonal crystals with the rhombohedral Bravais lattice and it is therefore important to know how to transform Miller indices and zone axis symbols from one axis system to the other. The appropriate matrix equations or **transformation matrices** are given in Appendix 4. However, the concept and derivation of transformation matrices are best understood by way of an easily visualized, in effect, 'two-dimensional' example (Fig. 5.9) in which one of the axes out of the plane of the paper is common to both cells.

Figure 5.9 shows a plan view of a lattice with two possible unit cells outlined by vectors **a**, **b**, **c** and **A**, **B**, **C**. The common vectors **c** = **C** lie out of the plane of the paper. The unit cell vectors **A**, **B**, **C** can be expressed as components of **a**, **b**, **c**:

$$\mathbf{A} = 1\mathbf{a} + 2\mathbf{b} + 0\mathbf{c}$$
$$\mathbf{B} = \bar{1}\mathbf{a} + 1\mathbf{b} + 0\mathbf{c}$$
$$\mathbf{C} = 0\mathbf{a} + 0\mathbf{b} + 1\mathbf{c}.$$

Now there are two ways of writing these three equations in matrix form; the vectors may either be written as column matrices:

$$\begin{pmatrix} \mathbf{A} \\ \mathbf{B} \\ \mathbf{C} \end{pmatrix} = \begin{pmatrix} 1 & 2 & 0 \\ \bar{1} & 1 & 0 \\ 0 & 0 & 1 \end{pmatrix} \begin{pmatrix} \mathbf{a} \\ \mathbf{b} \\ \mathbf{c} \end{pmatrix}$$

or as row matrices:

$$(\mathbf{A}\,\mathbf{B}\,\mathbf{C}) = (\mathbf{a}\,\mathbf{b}\,\mathbf{c}) \begin{pmatrix} 1 & \bar{1} & 0 \\ 2 & 1 & 0 \\ 0 & 0 & 1 \end{pmatrix}.$$

Notice that the rows and columns of the 3×3 matrix are transposed.

Let (hkl) and $[uvw]$ be the Miller indices and zone axis symbols referred to the primitive unit cell $\mathbf{a}, \mathbf{b}, \mathbf{c}$ and (HKL) and $[UVW]$ be the Miller indices and zone axis symbols referred to the 'large' unit cell $\mathbf{A}, \mathbf{B}, \mathbf{C}$ (which has three lattice points per cell).

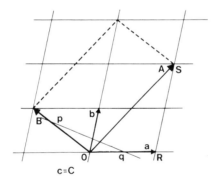

Fig. 5.9. Alternative unit cells in a lattice defined by unit cell vectors $\mathbf{a}, \mathbf{b}, \mathbf{c}$ and $\mathbf{A}, \mathbf{B}, \mathbf{C}$.

Consider first the transformation between the indices (hkl) and (HKL). Figure 5.9 shows the trace pq of the first plane from the origin in a family of planes in the lattice. By definition, the intercepts of this plane are a/h on the $\mathbf{a}$ lattice vector, A/H on the $\mathbf{B}$ lattice vector, b/k on the $\mathbf{b}$ lattice vector and so on. Or, recall the equivalent definition that h is the number of planes intersected along the $\mathbf{a}$ lattice vector, H is the number intersected along the $\mathbf{A}$ lattice vector, and so on; h is the number intersected along $\mathbf{a}$ (i.e. 0 to R) and $2k$ is the number intersected along $2\mathbf{b}$ (i.e. R to S). Hence, $h + 2k$ is the total number of planes intersected along $1\mathbf{a} + 2\mathbf{b}$ (i.e. 0 to S) and, as $\mathbf{A} = 1\mathbf{a} + 2\mathbf{b}$, then this number is the H index. Hence

$$H = 1h + 2k + 0l$$
$$K = \bar{1}h + 1k + 0l$$
$$L = 0h + 0k + 1l,$$

and the indices transform in the same way as the unit cell vectors, and again can be written in matrix form as column matrices or row matrices. We shall choose the *row* matrix form, viz.

$$(HKL) = (hkl) \begin{pmatrix} 1 & \bar{1} & 0 \\ 2 & 1 & 0 \\ 0 & 0 & 1 \end{pmatrix}.$$

The relationship between $[uvw]$ and $[UVW]$ may be derived as follows. A vector $\mathbf{r}$ in the lattice is written in terms of its components on the two sets of lattice vectors, i.e.

$$\mathbf{r} = u\mathbf{a} + v\mathbf{b} + w\mathbf{c} = U\mathbf{A} + V\mathbf{B} + W\mathbf{C}.$$

Substituting for $\mathbf{A}$, $\mathbf{B}$ and $\mathbf{C}$:

$$U\mathbf{a} + v\mathbf{b} + w\mathbf{c} = U(1\mathbf{a} + 2\mathbf{b} + 0\mathbf{c}) + V(\bar{1}\mathbf{a} + 1\mathbf{b} + 0\mathbf{c}) + W(0\mathbf{a} + 0\mathbf{b} + 1\mathbf{c}).$$

Collecting terms together for u, v and w gives

$$u = 1U + \bar{1}V + 0W$$
$$v = 2U + 1V + 0W$$
$$w = 0U + 0V + 1W.$$

Writing the zone axis symbols as *column* matrices gives

$$\begin{pmatrix} u \\ v \\ w \end{pmatrix} = \begin{pmatrix} 1 & \bar{1} & 0 \\ 2 & 1 & 0 \\ 0 & 0 & 1 \end{pmatrix} \begin{pmatrix} U \\ V \\ W \end{pmatrix}.$$

Hence the *same* 3×3 matrix relates plane indices written as *row* matrices from the primitive to 'large' unit cell and zone axis symbols written as column matrices from the 'large' to the primitive unit cell.

The reverse relationships are found from the inverse of the matrix. The procedures for inverting a matrix and for finding its determinant may be found in many A-level mathematics textbooks. For this example the inverse matrix is given by

$$\begin{pmatrix} 1 & \bar{1} & 0 \\ 2 & 1 & 0 \\ 0 & 0 & 1 \end{pmatrix}^{-1} = \tfrac{1}{3} \begin{pmatrix} 1 & 1 & 0 \\ \bar{2} & 1 & 0 \\ 0 & 0 & 3 \end{pmatrix};$$

hence

$$(h\,k\,l) = (HKL)\,\tfrac{1}{3} \begin{pmatrix} 1 & 1 & 0 \\ \bar{2} & 1 & 0 \\ 0 & 0 & 3 \end{pmatrix}.$$

and

$$\begin{pmatrix} U \\ V \\ W \end{pmatrix} = \tfrac{1}{3} \begin{pmatrix} \overline{1} & 1 & 0 \\ \overline{2} & 1 & 0 \\ 0 & 0 & 3 \end{pmatrix} \begin{pmatrix} u \\ v \\ w \end{pmatrix}.$$

Finally, note that the determinant of the matrix equals 3 (and its inverse equals $\tfrac{1}{3}$), the ratio of the volumes, or number of lattice points, in the unit cells.

In transforming indices and zone axis symbols from one set of crystal axes to another it is usually best to work from first principles as above because it is very easy to fall into error by using a transformation matrix without knowing which conventions for writing lattice planes and directions are being used.

Exercises

1. Write down the Miller indices and zone axis symbols for the slip planes and slip directions in fcc and bcc crystals. (See also Exercise 4, Chapter 1.)
2. Which of the directions [010], [432], [$\overline{2}$10], [23$\overline{1}$], if any, lie parallel to the plane (115)? Which of the planes (112), (321), (911$\overline{2}$), (1$\overline{1}$1), if any, lie parallel to the direction [1$\overline{1}\overline{1}$]?
3. Write down the planes whose normals are parallel to directions with the same numerical indices in the triclinic, monoclinic and tetragonal systems.
4. Find the plane which lies parallel to the directions [131] and [0$\overline{1}$1]. Find the plane which lies parallel to the directions [102] and [$\overline{1}$11]. Find the direction which lies parallel to the intersection of the planes (342) and (10$\overline{3}$). Find the direction which lies parallel to the intersection of the planes (21$\overline{3}$) and (110).
5. An orthorhombic crystal (cementite, Fe_3C) has unit cell vectors (or lattice parameters) of lengths $a = 452$ pm, $b = 508$ pm, $c = 674$ pm.
   (a) Find the d-spacings of the following families of planes: (101), (100), (111) and (202).
   (b) Find the angles α, β, γ (Fig. 5.6) between the normal to the plane (111) and the three crystal axes.
   (c) Find the angles p, q, r between the [111] direction and the three crystal axes. Briefly explain why these angles are not the same as those in (b).
6. Draw the directions (zone axes) [001], [010], [210], [110] in a hexagonal unit cell, and determine their Weber zone axis symbols, $\langle UVTW \rangle$.

6 The reciprocal lattice

6.1 Introduction

The **reciprocal lattice** is often regarded by students of physics as a geometrical abstraction, comprehensible only in terms of vector algebra and difficult diffraction theory. It is, in fact, a very simple concept and therefore a very important one. It provides a simple geometrical basis for understanding not only the geometry of X-ray and electron diffraction patterns but also the behaviour of electrons in crystals—reciprocal space being essentially identical to 'k-space'.

The concept of the reciprocal lattice may be approached in two ways, First, reciprocal lattice unit cell vectors may be defined in terms of the (direct) lattice unit cell vectors **a**, **b**, **c**, and the geometrical properties of the reciprocal lattice developed therefrom. This is certainly an elegant approach, but it very often fails to provide the student with an immediate understanding of the relationships, for example, between the reciprocal lattice of a crystal and the diffraction pattern. The second approach, which is the one adopted in this chapter, is much less elegant. It develops the notion that families of planes in crystals can be represented simply by their normals, which are then specified as (reciprocal lattice) vectors and which can then be used to define a pattern of (reciprocal lattice) points, each (reciprocal lattice) point representing a family of planes. The advantage of this approach is that it accentuates the connections between families of planes in the crystals, Bragg's Law and the directions of the diffracted or reflected beams.

The notion that crystal axes can be defined in terms of the *normals* to crystal faces belongs to Bravais (1850) who called them 'polar axes' (not to be confused with current usage of the term which means axes or directions whose ends are not related by symmetry). However, the credit for the development of this idea to the concept of the reciprocal lattice, and the application of this concept to the analysis of X-ray diffraction patterns, belongs to P. P. Ewald*, a physicist who never achieved the recognition for his work that was his due. The story is briefly recorded in his autobiographical sketch in *50 Years of X-Ray Diffraction*.

Ewald was a 'doctorand'—a research student working in the Institute of Theoretical Physics in the University of Munich under Professor A. Sommerfeld. The subject of his thesis was 'To find the optical properties of an anisotropic arrangement of isotropic oscillators'. In January 1912, while

*Denotes biographical notes available in Appendix 3.

he was in the final stages of writing up his thesis he visited Max von Laue, a staff member of the Institute, to discuss some of the conclusions of his work. Ewald records that Laue listened to him in a slightly distracted way and insisted first on knowing what was the distance between the oscillators in Ewald's model; perhaps 1/500 or 1/1000 of the wavelength of light, Ewald suggested. Then Laue asked "what would happen if you assumed very much shorter waves to travel through the crystal?". Ewald turned to Paragraph 6, Formula 7, of his thesis manuscript, saying 'this formula shows the results of the superposition of all wavelets issuing from the resonators. It has been derived without any neglection or approximation and is therefore valid also for short wavelengths.' Ewald copied the formula down for Laue shortly before taking his leave, saying that he, Laue, was welcome to discuss it. Laue's question, of course, arose from his intuitive insight that if X-rays were waves and not particles, with wavelengths very much smaller than light, then they might be diffracted by such an array of regularly spaced oscillators.

The next Ewald heard of Laue's interest was through a report which Sommerfeld gave in June 1912 on the successful Laue–Friedrich–Knipping experiments. He realized that the formula which he had copied down for Laue, and which Laue had made no use of, provided the obvious way of interpreting the geometry of the diffraction patterns—by means of a construction which he called the reciprocal lattice and a sphere determined by the mode of incidence of the X-rays on the crystal (the Ewald or reflecting sphere). Ewald's interpretation of the geometry of X-ray diffraction was not published until 1913, by which time rapid progress in crystal structure analysis had already been made by W. H. and W. L. Bragg in Leeds and Cambridge.

6.2 Reciprocal lattice vectors

Consider a family of planes in a crystal (for example, those in Figures 5.2 or 5.3). Geometrically the planes can be specified by two quantities: (1) their orientation in the crystal and (2) their d-spacing. Now, the orientation of the planes is defined by the direction of their normal. In Figure 6.1(a) two families of planes, labelled 1 and 2, are sketched 'edge on'. It is immaterial where the crystal axes are in relation to these planes, so they are omitted. In Figure 6.1(b), the normals to these planes are drawn from a common origin and these specify the orientation of the planes. Now the d-spacings, d_1 and d_2 need to be specified. An 'obvious' way of doing this might be to make the lengths of the normals directly proportional to the d-spacings, i.e. by expressing them as vectors with moduli equal to $K \times (d\text{-spacing})$ where K is a proportionality constant. However, this is *not* the way; instead, we make the lengths or the moduli of the vectors *inversely* proportional to the d-spacings, i.e. equal to K/d-spacing (where K is a proportionality constant, taken as unity or in X-ray diffraction, as λ, the X-ray wavelength), i.e. a *longer* vector, indicating a *smaller* d-spacing. The reason for making the moduli of the

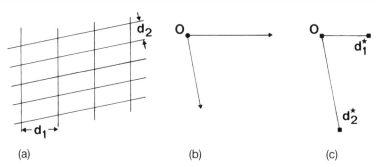

Fig. 6.1. (a) Traces of two families of planes 1 and 2 (perpendicular to the plane of the paper), (b) the normals to these families of planes drawn from a common origin and (c) definition of these planes in terms of the reciprocal (lattice) vectors $\mathbf{d}_1^*$ and $\mathbf{d}_2^*$, where $\mathbf{d}_1^* = K/d_1$, $\mathbf{d}_2^* = K/d_2$, K being a constant.

vectors inversely proportional to the *d*-spacings will be apparent shortly (recall also the inversion of the intercepts in the definition of Miller indices). These vectors are called **reciprocal (lattice) vectors**, symbols $\mathbf{d}_1^*$ and $\mathbf{d}_2^*$, and are shown in Figure 6.1(c). The 'end points' of the vectors (called reciprocal lattice points) are labelled 1 and 2, corresponding to the planes which they represent. Reciprocal lattice vectors have dimensions of 1/length (for $K = 1$), e.g. reciprocal ångströms, Å^{-1}, or reciprocal picometres, pm^{-1}. For example, if $d_1 = 0.5$ Å, the length or modulus of $\mathbf{d}_1^*$ (for $K = 1$) is

$$|\mathbf{d}_1^*| = \frac{1}{0.5 \text{ Å}} = 2 \text{ Å}^{-1}.$$

This completes the simple definition of reciprocal lattice vectors. But, like all simple concepts, it is capable of great development, which will be done for particular examples in the sections below. First a practical note. In drawing crystals and in sketching crystal planes we have to use a 'map scale' in 'direct space', choosing a scale to fit our piece of paper, e.g. 1 Å equals 1 cm. So also when drawing reciprocal lattice vectors we have to use a quite separate 'map scale' in 'reciprocal space', e.g. 1 Å^{-1} equals 1 cm or 10 cm or 1 inch, as convenient.

6.3 Reciprocal lattice unit cells

To avoid the pitfalls of making hasty assumptions about the relationships between reciprocal and (direct) lattice vectors, a monoclinic crystal will be used as an example. First, we shall draw the reciprocal lattice vectors in a section perpendicular to the *y*-axis (i.e. containing the **a** and **c** lattice vectors) from which we will find the reciprocal lattice unit cell vectors **a*** and **c***. This then enables us to express reciprocal lattice vectors in this section in terms of their components on these vectors. It is then a simple step to extend these ideas to three dimensions.

Figure 6.2(a) shows a section of a monoclinic P lattice through the origin and perpendicular to the y-axis or **b** unit cell vector. The section of the unit cell is outlined by the lattice vectors **a** and **c** at the obtuse angle β and also the traces of some planes of the type $(h0l)$ (i.e. those planes parallel to the y-axis). In Figure 6.2(a) [and Fig. 6.4(a)] no distinction is made between Miller indices and Laue indices—the indices of the planes are all put in brackets whether or not they all pass through lattice points.

Figures 6.2(b) and (c) show the reciprocal lattice vectors for these planes, with the reciprocal lattice points labelled with the index of the planes they represent. Note again the reciprocal relationships between the lengths of the vectors and the d-spacings, e.g. the (002) planes with half the d-spacing of the (001) planes are represented by a reciprocal lattice point 002, twice the distance from the origin as the reciprocal lattice point 001. Obviously, 003 will be three times the distance, and so on.

It can be seen that the reciprocal lattice points (the 'end points' of the reciprocal lattice vectors) do indeed form a grid or lattice—hence the name. This is emphasized in Figure 6.2(c), which also shows the **reciprocal lattice unit cell** for this section outlined by reciprocal lattice cell vectors **a*** and **c***, where

$$\mathbf{a}^* = \mathbf{d}^*_{100} \quad \text{and} \quad |\mathbf{a}^*| = 1/d_{100}; \quad \mathbf{c}^* = \mathbf{d}^*_{001} \quad \text{and} \quad |\mathbf{c}^*| = 1/d_{001}.$$

Note that **a*** and **c*** are *not* parallel to **a** and **c** respectively because the normals to the (100) and (001) planes in the monoclinic lattice are not parallel to **a** and **c** respectively. Also the angle β^* between **a*** and **c*** is the complement of the angle β.

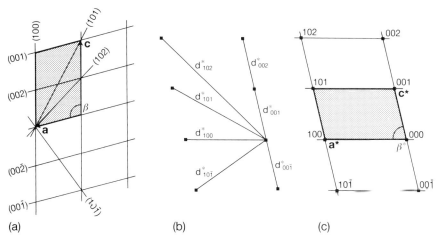

(a)   (b)   (c)

Fig. 6.2. (a) Plan of a monoclinic P unit cell perpendicular to the y-axis with the unit cell shaded. The traces of some planes of type $\{h0l\}$ (i.e. parallel to the y-axis) are indicated, (b) the reciprocal (lattice) vectors, $\mathbf{d}^*_{hkl}$ for these planes and (c) the reciprocal lattice defined by these vectors. Each reciprocal lattice point is labelled with the indices of the plane it represents and the unit cell is shaded. The angle β^* is the complement of β.

These ideas are readily extended to the third dimension; the **b*** vector is perpendicular to the plane of the paper, normal to the (010) planes which are parallel to the plane of the paper, i.e. in the monoclinic system **b** is parallel to **b***.

The reciprocal lattice vectors can now be expressed in terms of their components on the reciprocal unit cell vectors **a***, **b***, **c***. For example, for the (102) family of planes [Figs 6.2(b) and (c)] $\mathbf{d}^*_{102} = 1\mathbf{a}^* + 0\mathbf{b}^* + 2\mathbf{c}^*$, or, in general,

$$\mathbf{d}^*_{hkl} = h\mathbf{a}^* + k\mathbf{b}^* + l\mathbf{c}^*.$$

Hence, just as direction symbols [*uvw*] are the components of a vector $\mathbf{r}_{uvw}$ in direct space (Chapter 5.2), so also plane indices are the components of a vector $\mathbf{d}^*_{hkl}$ in reciprocal space.

The reciprocal unit cell of the monoclinic crystal is sketched in Figure 6.3. Note that each corner represents a family of planes and is labelled with the appropriate plane index and that the origin is labelled 000.

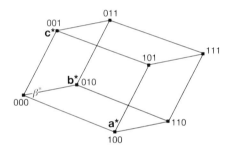

Fig. 6.3. The reciprocal lattice unit cell of a monoclinic *P* crystal defined by reciprocal lattice vectors **a***, **b*** and **c***. β^* is the angle between **a*** and **c***.

6.4 Some geometrical relationships

Some geometrical relationships, stated without proof in Chapter 5, can be proved very simply using the reciprocal lattice. Elementary knowledge of vector algebra will also be assumed. The results are summarized in Appendix 4.

6.4.1 The (Weiss) zone law

If a plane (*hkl*) lies in a zone [*uvw*], then $\mathbf{d}^*_{hkl}$ is perpendicular to $\mathbf{r}_{uvw}$, i.e. $\mathbf{d}^*_{hkl} \cdot \mathbf{r}_{uvw} = 0$. Writing $\mathbf{d}^*_{hkl}$ and $\mathbf{r}_{uvw}$ in terms of their components,

$$(h\mathbf{a}^* + k\mathbf{b}^* + l\mathbf{c}^*) \cdot (u\mathbf{a} + v\mathbf{b} + w\mathbf{c}) = 0.$$

Hence

$$hu + kv + lw = 0 \quad \text{because } \mathbf{a}^* \cdot \mathbf{a} = 1, \mathbf{a}^* \cdot \mathbf{b} = 0, \text{etc.}$$

The zone law can be generalized as follows. Consider the condition for a lattice point with co-ordinates uvw (or with position vector $\mathbf{r}_{uvw}$) to lie in a lattice plane (hkl). For the lattice plane passing through the origin, $\mathbf{r}_{uvw}$ is perpendicular to $\mathbf{d}^*_{hkl}$ and hence $hu + kv + lw = 0$ as before. Now consider the nth lattice plane which lies at a perpendicular distance nd_{hkl} from the origin. The condition for a lattice point to be in this plane is that the component of $\mathbf{r}_{uvw}$ perpendicular to the planes should equal this distance; i.e. $\mathbf{r}_{uvw} \cdot \mathbf{i} = nd_{hkl}$ where $\mathbf{i}$ is a unit vector perpendicular to the planes. As

$$\mathbf{i} = \frac{\mathbf{d}^*_{hkl}}{|\mathbf{d}^*_{hkl}|} = \mathbf{d}^*_{hkl} d_{hkl}$$

then

$$\mathbf{r}_{uvw} \cdot \mathbf{d}^*_{hkl} d_{hkl} = nd_{hkl};$$

hence

$$\mathbf{r}_{uvw} \cdot \mathbf{d}^*_{hkl} = n$$

and, substituting for $\mathbf{r}_{uvw}$ and $\mathbf{d}^*_{hkl}$ as before,

$$hu + kv + lw = n.$$

6.4.2 Relationships between *a*, *b*, *c* and *a**, *b**, *c**

Consider, for example, $\mathbf{c}^*$ [Fig. 6.2(c)]. As $\mathbf{c}^*$ is perpendicular to $\mathbf{a}$ and $\mathbf{b}$, then $\mathbf{c}^* \cdot \mathbf{a} = 0$, $\mathbf{c}^* \cdot \mathbf{b} = 0$ and similarly for $\mathbf{a}^*$ and $\mathbf{b}^*$. Now $\mathbf{c} \cdot \mathbf{c}^* = c|\mathbf{c}^*| \cos \varphi$, where φ is the angle between $\mathbf{c}$ and $\mathbf{c}^*$. However, as $|\mathbf{c}^*| = 1/d_{001}$ by definition and $c \cos \varphi = d_{001}$, then $\mathbf{c} \cdot \mathbf{c}^* = 1$ and similarly $\mathbf{a} \cdot \mathbf{a}^* = \mathbf{b} \cdot \mathbf{b}^* = 1$.

6.4.3 The addition rule

This rule is simply based on the addition of reciprocal lattice vectors. For example [Fig. 6.2(b)], $\mathbf{d}^*_{102} = \mathbf{d}^*_{101} + \mathbf{d}^*_{001}$ or, in general,

$$\mathbf{d}^*_{(mh_1 + nh_2)(mk_1 + nk_2)(ml_1 + nl_2)} = \mathbf{d}^*_{m(h_1 k_1 l_1)} + \mathbf{d}^*_{n(h_2 k_2 l_2)}.$$

6.4.4 Definition of *a**, *b**, *c** in terms of *a*, *b*, *c*

The volume of the unit cell V is given by $\mathbf{a} \cdot (\mathbf{b} \times \mathbf{c})$. Now, as $(\mathbf{b} \times \mathbf{c})$ is a vector parallel to $\mathbf{a}^*$ and of modulus equal to the area of the face of the unit cell defined by $\mathbf{b}$ and $\mathbf{c}$, then $\mathbf{a}^* = (\mathbf{b} \times \mathbf{c})/V = (\mathbf{b} \times \mathbf{c})/\mathbf{a} \cdot (\mathbf{b} \times \mathbf{c})$, and similarly for $\mathbf{a}^*$ and $\mathbf{c}^*$. $\mathbf{a}$, $\mathbf{b}$ and $\mathbf{c}$ can be defined in the same way, i.e. $\mathbf{a} = (\mathbf{b}^* \times \mathbf{c}^*)/V^*$, and similarly for $\mathbf{b}$ and $\mathbf{c}$, where V^* is the volume of the reciprocal unit cell.

6.4.5 Zone axis at intersection of planes $(h_1k_1l_1)$ and $(h_2k_2l_2)$

The zone axis is defined by $\mathbf{r}_{uvw}$, the vector product of

$$\mathbf{d}^*_{h_1k_1l_1} \text{ and } \mathbf{d}^*_{h_2k_2l_2}.$$

Substituting in terms of their components and remembering the identities $\mathbf{a} = (\mathbf{b}^* \times \mathbf{c}^*)/V^*$, etc., gives

$$u\mathbf{a} + v\mathbf{b} + w\mathbf{c} = \mathbf{a}(k_1l_2 - k_2l_1) + \mathbf{b}(l_1h_2 - l_2h_1) + \mathbf{c}(h_1k_2 - h_2k_1)$$

therefore

$$u = (k_1l_2 - k_2l_1); \quad v = (l_1h_2 - l_2h_1); \quad w = (h_1k_2 - h_2k_1).$$

6.4.6 A plane containing two directions $[u_1v_1w_1]$ and $[u_2v_2w_2]$

The plane is defined by $\mathbf{d}^*_{hkl}$, the vector product of $\mathbf{r}_{u_1v_1w_1}$ and $\mathbf{r}_{u_2v_2w_2}$. Proceeding as above gives

$$h = (v_1w_2 - v_2w_1); \quad k = (w_1u_2 - w_2u_1); \quad l = (u_1v_2 - u_2v_1).$$

6.4.7 d-Spacing of planes (hkl)

$$\frac{1}{\mathbf{d}_{hkl}} = |\mathbf{d}^*_{hkl}| = \sqrt{(\mathbf{d}^*_{hkl} \cdot \mathbf{d}^*_{hkl})}.$$

Substitute for $\mathbf{d}^*_{hkl}$ in terms of $h\mathbf{a}^* + k\mathbf{b}^* + l\mathbf{c}^*$. Simple expressions are obtained only for crystals with orthogonal axes (orthorhombic, tetragonal, cubic) where $\mathbf{a}^* \cdot \mathbf{b}^* = 0$, etc.

6.4.8 Angle ρ between plane normals $h_1k_1l_1$ and $h_2k_2l_2$

$$\cos\rho = \frac{\mathbf{d}^*_{h_1k_1l_1} \cdot \mathbf{d}^*_{h_2k_2l_2}}{|\mathbf{d}^*_{h_1k_1l_1}||\mathbf{d}^*_{h_2k_2l_2}|}.$$

Again, substituting in terms of components gives a simple expression only for cubic crystals.

6.5 Reciprocal lattice cells for cubic crystals

In crystals with orthogonal axes (cubic, tetragonal, orthorhombic) the reciprocal lattice vectors $\mathbf{a}^*$, $\mathbf{b}^*$, $\mathbf{c}^*$ are parallel to $\mathbf{a}$, $\mathbf{b}$, $\mathbf{c}$, respectively. Hence we have the further identities that $\mathbf{a} \cdot \mathbf{b} = 0$, $\mathbf{a}^* \cdot \mathbf{b}^* = 0$, etc. The reciprocal lattice unit cell of a simple cubic crystal (cubic P lattice) is obviously a cube with reciprocal lattice points only at the corners. But the reciprocal unit cells of the cubic *I* and cubic *F* lattices also have additional lattice points within the unit cells, i.e. they are also not primitive. This is illustrated for the case of the cubic *I* lattice in Figure 6.4, which shows two unit cells with the *z*-axis perpendicular to the plane of the paper and the traces of several $hk0$ planes (parallel to the *z*-axis) sketched in. Notice (for example) that in the direction of the *x*-axis the first set of *lattice* planes encountered is not (100) but (200) because of the presence of the additional lattice points in the centres of the cells (see also Figure 5.4). Hence the reciprocal lattice vector in this direction is equal to $\mathbf{d}^*_{200}$ not $\mathbf{d}^*_{100}$; similarly, in the direction of the *y*-axis it is $\mathbf{d}^*_{020}$. In the [110] direction, however, the first set of lattice planes encountered is (110), which gives a reciprocal lattice point in the centre of the face of the cell and the second-order 220 reciprocal lattice point at the corner. Proceeding in this way we find that this section of the reciprocal lattice is *face-centred*. Repeating this procedure in the other sections gives a **face-centred cubic reciprocal lattice (cubic *F*)** (Fig. 6.5) for the **body-centred cubic (direct) lattice (cubic *I*)**—the two are reciprocally related. In the same way, we find that the reciprocal lattice of the face-centred cubic lattice is body-centred (Fig. 6.6).

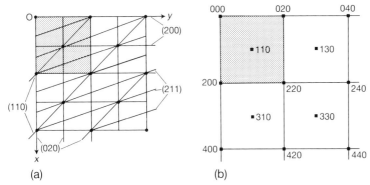

Fig. 6.4. (a) Plan of a cubic *I* crystal perpendicular to the *z*-axis and (b) pattern of reciprocal lattice points perpendicular to the *z*-axis. Note the cubic *F* arrangement of reciprocal lattice points in this plane.

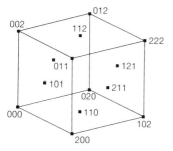

Fig. 6.5. The cubic *F* reciprocal lattice unit cell of the cubic *I* (direct) lattice.

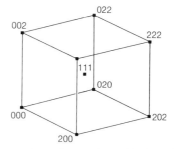

Fig. 6.6. The cubic *I* recriprocal lattice cell of the cubic *F* (direct) lattice.

There is another way of looking at these reciprocal relationships. Recall that the cubic lattices may all be referred to rhombohedral axes (primitive cells) with axial angles of 60° (cubic *F*), 90° (cubic *P*), and 109.47° (cubic *I*) (Section 3.3, Fig. 3.2). The reciprocals of these cells are again rhombohedral cells with axial angles 109.47° (i.e. cubic *I*), 90° (i.e. cubic *P*) and 60° (i.e. cubic *F*) respectively.

Exercises

1. Derive the [0001] reciprocal lattice section for the hexagonal *P* lattice and the [111] reciprocal lattice sections for the cubic *I* and cubic *F* lattices.
2. Derive expressions for $1/\mathbf{d}_{hkl}$ and cos ρ for orthorhombic crystals.
3. Do the relationships derived in Section 6.5 apply also to non-cubic centred Bravais lattices and their reciprocal unit cells?

7 The diffraction of light, X-rays and electrons: applications of the reciprocal lattice in diffraction

7.1 Introduction

As mentioned in Chapter 6, the concept of the reciprocal lattice and the reflecting sphere and their applications in determining the direction of the diffracted beams from crystals (and hence the geometry of diffraction patterns) was the major achievement of P. P. Ewald. As we shall see in Section 7.6, the electron diffraction patterns observed in the electron microscope are simply sections through the reciprocal lattice of the crystal perpendicular, or nearly perpendicular, to the direction of the electron beam—the pattern of spots on the screen or photographic film and the pattern of reciprocal lattice points are identical. This also applies to the diffraction of light from 'two-dimensional crystals' such as fine woven fabrics—umbrella cloths, window net curtains and the like—in which the warp and weft of the cloth correspond to intersecting lattice planes (Section 7.2).

The reciprocal lattice therefore is not merely a geometrical abstraction, a formal way of representing lattice planes in crystals or two-dimensional nets: it is something which we can 'see for ourselves'. Indeed, in the case of the diffraction of light, it is a familiar part of our everyday visual sensations.

The geometrical similarity between light and electron diffraction arises because in both cases the wavelengths of light and electrons are small in comparison with the fibre or line separations in woven fabrics or the lattice spacings in crystals, respectively. The diffraction angles in both cases therefore are also small (Sections 7.2 and 7.6). A consideration of diffraction of light from nets or woven fabrics (Section 7.2) is justified partly because of its familiarity and partly because of its analogy with electron diffraction.

The geometry of X-ray diffraction patterns is rather more complicated because (unlike electrons in the electron microscope) the wavelengths of X-rays are roughly comparable with the lattice spacings in crystals. Hence the diffraction angles are large (Sections 7.3 and 7.4). X-ray diffraction patterns of crystals are in a sense often 'distorted' representations of their reciprocal lattices, the nature of the 'distortion' depending upon the particular X-ray technique used: i.e. whether polychromatic (or 'white' X-radiation) or monochromatic (or filtered) X-radiation is used; whether the

79

crystal is oscillated, rotated or precessed; and whether the patterns are recorded on flat, curved, stationary or moving films.

Detailed considerations of X-ray and electron diffraction techniques are beyond the scope of this handbook. However, all techniques are based upon the underlying principles of the reciprocal lattice and the reflecting sphere construction, a firm understanding of which is essential and which is best approached by considering first the approach of Laue (Section 7.3), and then that of W. L. Bragg (Section 7.4) to the analysis of X-ray diffraction patterns. The equations are written in both scalar and vector notation. Readers unfamiliar with vector notation should refer to Appendix 5.

Finally, it should be pointed out that the words 'diffraction' and 'diffraction pattern' are inadequate as descriptions of the physical processes involved since they imply that the patterns observed are simply the consequence of a diffraction or scattering process—whether by atoms (X-rays or electrons) or at the edges of opaque obstacles (light). A much better description of the phenomena would be 'diffraction–interference' which indicates that the patterns arise (a) as a result of scattering or diffraction by atoms or obstacles and (b) by the processes of interference between these scattered beams—the nature of the interference depending upon the path differences between them. However, the words 'diffraction pattern' are so ingrained in the literature that it is doubtful whether they will ever be replaced by 'diffraction–interference pattern'.

7.2 The diffraction of light

In order to observe and record the diffraction of light, two things are required—a point source of light and a piece of fabric with an open weave. A point source of light may in practice be a distant street lamp or, in order to conduct the experiments indoors, a mini torch bulb or a domestic light bulb placed behind a screen with a pinhole (or a fine needle hole) punched into it. Nylon net curtain material is an effective fabric to use—the filaments of nylon which make up the strands are tightly twisted giving sharply defined transparent/opaque boundaries and there are clear spaces inbetween about equal in width to the strands.

Observe the point source (which should be at least 5 m distant) through the net. The image of the point source will be seen to be repeated to form a grid (or reciprocal lattice) of diffraction spots [Fig. 7.1(a)]. In general the spots are of greatest intensity, and are streaked, in directions perpendicular to the lines or strands of the net.

These familiar observations may be supplemented by two more. Firstly the same pattern of spots is seen whether both, or only one, eye is used. Secondly the size of the pattern—the apparent spacing of the spots—is *independent* of the position of the net. The diffraction pattern appears to be unchanged, irrespective of whether the net is held away from, or close to the

Fig. 7.1. (a) A diffraction pattern from a piece of net curtain with a square weave. The outline of the net is indicated by the white frame. Note the two rows of strong spots and the fainter spots forming a square grid diffraction pattern. (b) The diffraction pattern is identical in scale when the net is brought closer to the observer's eye. (c) Rotating the net about a vertical axis reduces the effective spacing of the vertical lines of the weave, resulting in diffraction spots in the horizontal direction which are further apart. (d) Shearing or distorting the net such that the strands or lines are no longer at 90° to each other results in a diffraction pattern 'sheared' in the opposite sense—the rows of strong diffraction spots remain perpendicular to the lines of the net.

eyes [Fig. 7.1(b)]*. These observations show that the diffraction spots or diffracted beams bear fixed angular relationships to the direct beam.

The reciprocal relationship between the net and diffraction pattern may be demonstrated in two ways. Firstly, a net with a finer line spacing will be found to give diffraction spots more widely spaced. If a finer net is not available, the effective spacing of the lines may be decreased by rotating the net such that it is no longer orientated perpendicular to the line of sight to the light [Fig. 7.1(c)]. Secondly, the net may be twisted or sheared such that the strands—the weft and the warp—no longer lie in lines at 90° to each other. It will be seen that the rows of strong diffraction spots rotate in such a way that

*If the light falling on the net is not parallel but is slightly diverging (i.e. the point source is not effectively at infinity), then the apparent spacing of the spots will change slightly as the net is held at different distances from the eyes.

they continue to lie in directions perpendicular to the lines of the net—the grid of diffraction spots is reciprocally related to the sheared lattice [Fig. 7.1(d)].

These reciprocal relationships are analogous to those shown for a set of planes in a zone parallel to the *y*-axis in a monoclinic crystal [corresponding to the net, Fig. 6.2(a)] and its reciprocal lattice section [corresponding to the diffraction pattern, Fig. 6.2(c)]. These very important conclusions will be made clearer by considering the conditions for constructive interference in the diffracted light from the net, which may be regarded as a two-dimensional diffraction grating.

Figure 7.2 shows one set of strands or row of lines of the net running perpendicularly to the page with parallel light incident on the row from the left. As discussed in Section 7.7 below, each slit between the strands may be regarded as the source of a single set of Huygens' wavelets spreading out cylindrically in all directions. Strong diffracted beams occur when the path difference between the wavelets scattered from adjacent slits is a whole number of wavelengths, i.e. $AB = a \sin \alpha_n = n\lambda$ where $a =$ the line (or lattice) spacing and α_n is the diffracted angle of the *n*th order diffracted beam. Since $\lambda \approx 0.5$ μm and typically $a = \approx 1$–2 mm, then the diffraction angles are small (because $a \gg \lambda$) and $\sin \alpha_n = \alpha_n$. Hence for the first few visible diffraction orders the path difference $AB = a\alpha_n = n\lambda$, hence $\alpha_n = n\lambda/a$, here we have the reciprocal relationship between the diffraction angles and the lattice spacing.

The analysis may be extended to the other set of lines in the net, giving a second set of diffracted beams. The observed diffracted spots lie at the intersections of the two sets of beams, forming a reciprocal lattice grid.

Although Fig. 7.2 is satisfactory for showing the path differences between the diffracted beams, it does not show the full geometry of the diffraction

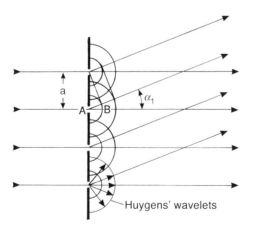

Fig. 7.2. A set of lines in the net acts as a diffraction grating, each slit acting as the source of a single net of Huygens' wavelets. The diffracted beam is drawn for a path difference of one wavelength.

pattern in relation to the observer's eye and in particular the effect of moving the net [Figs. 7.1(a) and (b)].

Figure 7.3 shows a parallel beam of light from a (distant) source with the net held away from the eye [Fig. 7.3(a)] and closer to the eye [(Fig. 7.3(b)]. One set of diffracted beams from the net is shown. Of all the direct light and diffracted light from the net, only a portion will enter the eye. The portion of the net from which the diffracted light entering the eye originates changes as the net is moved: the further the net is moved away from the eye the greater the contribution from its outer regions [compare Fig. 7.3(a) with Fig 7.3)b)]. However, for incident parallel light, irrespective of the position of the net, the angular relationship at the eye between the direct and diffracted beams, and hence the apparent size of the diffraction pattern, remains unchanged.

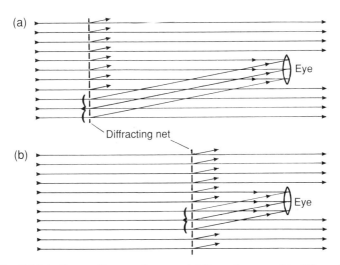

Fig. 7.3. Parallel light (from a distant point source) falls on the net and is diffracted; only one set of diffracted beams is shown. The region of the net contributing to the diffracted light entering the eye of the observer is indicated by brackets. (b) As the net is moved towards the eye, the region of the net which contributes to the diffracted light entering the eye is different. The angular relationship between the direct and diffracted light at the eye remains unchanged.

7.3 Laue's analysis of X-ray diffraction: the three Laue equations

Laue's analysis of the geometry of X-ray diffraction patterns has been referred to in Section 5.5. What follows is a much simplified treatment which does not take into consideration Laue's interpretation of the origin of the diffracted waves from irradiated crystals.

Consider a simple crystal in which the motif is one atom and the atoms are simply to be regarded as scattering centres situated at lattice points. The more general situation in which the motif consists of more than one atom and in which the different scattering amplitudes of the atoms and the path differences between the atoms have to be taken into account is discussed in Section 7.7. The crystal may be considered to be built up of rows of atoms in three dimensions: rows of atoms of spacing a along the x-axis, of spacing b along the y-axis and of spacing c along the z-axis. Consider first of all the condition for constructive interference for the waves scattered from the row of atoms along the x-axis—which may simply be reduced to a consideration of the path differences between waves scattered from adjacent atoms in the row [Fig. 7.4(a)].

For constructive interference the path difference $(AB - CD)$ must be a whole number of wavelengths, i.e.

$$(AB - CD) = a(\cos \alpha_n - \cos \alpha_0) = n_x\lambda$$

where α_n, α_0 are the angles between the diffracted and incident beams to the x-axis respectively and n_x is an integer (the order of diffraction).

This equation, known as the First Laue Equation, may be expressed more elegantly in vector notation. Let $\mathbf{s}$, $\mathbf{s}_0$ be unit vectors along the directions of the diffracted and incident beams respectively, and let $\mathbf{a}$ be the translation vector from one lattice point (or atom position) to the next [Fig. 7.4(b)]. The path difference $a(\cos \alpha_n - \cos \alpha_0)$ may be represented by the scalar product $\mathbf{a} \cdot \mathbf{s} - \mathbf{a} \cdot \mathbf{s}_0 = \mathbf{a} \cdot (\mathbf{s} - \mathbf{s}_0)$. Hence the First Laue Equation may be written

$$a(\cos \alpha_n - \cos \alpha_0) = \mathbf{a} \cdot (\mathbf{s} - \mathbf{s}_0) = n_x\lambda.$$

Now Fig. 7.4 is misleading in that it only shows the diffracted beam at angle α_n **below** the atom row—but the same path difference obtains if the diffracted beam lies in the plane of the paper at angle α_n **above** the atom row— or indeed **out of the plane of the paper** at angle α_n to the atom row. Hence all the diffracted beams with the same path difference occur at the same angle to the atom row, i.e. the diffracted beams of the same order all lie on the surface of a cone—called a Laue cone—centred on the atom row with semi-apex angle α_n. This situation is illustrated in Fig. 7.5 which shows just three Laue cones with semi-apex angle α_0 (zero order, $n_x = 0$), semi-apex angle α_1 (first-order, $n_x = 1$) and semi-apex angle α_2 (second-order, $n_x = 2$). Clearly there

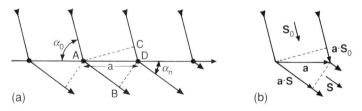

Fig. 7.4. (a) Diffraction from a lattice row along the x-axis. The incident and diffracted beams are at angles α_0 and α_n to the row. The path difference between the diffracted beams = $(AB - CD)$. (b) The incident and diffracted beam directions and the path difference between the diffracted beams expressed in vector notation.

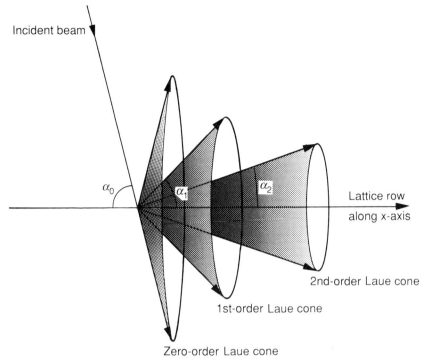

Fig. 7.5. Three Laue cones representing the directions of the diffracted beams from a lattice row along the x-axis with 0λ ($n_x = 0$), 1λ ($n_x = 1$) and 2λ ($n_x = 2$) path differences.

will be a whole set of such cones with semi-apex angles α_n varying between $0°$ and $180°$.

The analysis is now repeated for the atom row along the y-axis, giving the Second Laue Equation:

$$b \cos \beta_n - b \cos \beta_0 = \mathbf{b} \cdot (\mathbf{s} - \mathbf{s}_0) = n_y \lambda,$$

and for the atom row along the z-axis giving the Third Laue Equation:

$$c(\cos \gamma_n - \cos \gamma_0) = \mathbf{c}(\mathbf{s} - \mathbf{s}_0) = n_z \lambda,$$

where the angles β_n, β_0, γ_n, γ_0 and the integers n_y and n_z are defined in the same way as for α_n, α_0 and n_x.

Now, for constructive interference to occur simultaneously from all three atom rows, all three Laue Equations must be satisfied simultaneously. This is equivalent to the geometrical condition that diffracted beams only occur in those directions along which three Laue cones, centred along the x-, y- and z-axes, intersect. Each diffracted beam may be identified by three integers n_x, n_y and n_z which, as pointed out above, represent the order of diffraction from each of the atom rows. We shall find in Section 7.4 that these integers are simply the h, k and l Laue indices (see Section 5.5) of the reflecting planes in the crystal.

7.4 Bragg's analysis of X-ray diffraction: Bragg's Law

Laue's analysis is in effect an extension of the idea of a diffraction grating to three dimensions. It suffers from the severe practical disadvantage that in order to calculate the directions of the diffracted beams, a total of six angles α_n, α_0, β_n, β_0 and γ_n, γ_0; three lattice spacings a, b and c, and three integers n_x, n_y and n_z need to be determined. As discussed in Section 5.5, W.L. Bragg envisaged diffraction in terms of reflections from crystal planes giving rise to the simple relationship (Bragg's Law, derived below):

$$n\lambda = 2d_{hkl} \sin \theta.$$

It can be seen immediately, by comparing the Laue Equations with Bragg's Law, that the number of variables needed to calculate the directions of the diffracted beams are much reduced.

Bragg's Law may be derived with reference to Fig. 7.6(a) which shows (as for the derivation of the Laue equations) a simple crystal with one atom at each lattice point. The path difference between the waves scattered by atoms from adjacent (hkl) lattice planes of spacing d_{hkl} is given by $(AB + BC) = (d_{hkl} \sin \theta + d_{hkl} \sin \theta) = 2d_{hkl} \sin \theta$. Hence for constructive interference:

$$n\lambda = 2d_{hkl} \sin \theta,$$

where n is an integer (the order of reflection or diffraction).

As explained in Section 5.5, n is normally incorporated into the lattice plane symbol, i.e.

$$\lambda = 2 \left(\frac{d_{hkl}}{n} \right) \sin \theta = 2d_{nh\,nk\,nl} \sin \theta$$

where $nh\ nk\ nl$ are the Laue indices for the reflecting planes of spacing d_{hkl}/n.

Figure 7.6(a) represents a particularly simple geometrical situation in which the lattice is shown as a rectangular grid and the atoms are

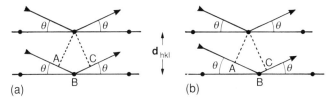

(a)　(b)

Fig. 7.6. (a) Bragg's Law for the case of a rectangular grid, i.e. $AB = BC = d_{hkl} \sin \theta$; the path difference $(AB + BC) = 2d_{hkl} \sin \theta$. (b) Bragg's Law for the general case in which $AB \neq BC$. Again, the path difference $(AB + BC) = 2d_{hkl} \sin \theta$.

symmetrically disposed with respect to the incident and diffracted beam, i.e.
AB = BC. Figure 7.6(b) shows a more general situation in which the lattice is
not rectangular and the distance AB does not equal BC. However, the sum
(AB + BC) is unchanged and is again equal to $2d_{hkl} \sin \theta$. The important
point is that Bragg's Law applies irrespective of the positions of the atoms
in the planes; it is solely the spacing between the planes which needs to
be considered. Finally, note that (unlike the Laue equations), Bragg's Law is
wholly represented in two dimensions—the incident and diffracted beams
and the normal to the reflecting planes (Fig. 7.6) all lie in a plane—i.e. the
plane of the paper.

Bragg's Law may also be expressed in vector notation. Again, let $\mathbf{s}$, $\mathbf{s}_0$ be
unit vectors along the directions of the diffracted and incident beams, then
(with reference to Fig. 7.7) the vector $(\mathbf{s} - \mathbf{s}_0)$ is parallel to $\mathbf{d}^*_{hkl}$, the reciprocal
lattice vector of the reflecting planes. Comparing the moduli of these vectors
$|\mathbf{s} - \mathbf{s}_0| = 2 \sin \theta$ and $|\mathbf{d}^*_{hkl}| = 1/d_{hkl}$, it is seen from Bragg's law that their ratio
is simply λ. Hence Bragg's Law may be written:

$$\frac{(\mathbf{s} - \mathbf{s}_0)}{\lambda} = \mathbf{d}^*_{hkl} = h\mathbf{a}^* + k\mathbf{b}^* + l\mathbf{c}^*.$$

Hence constructive interference occurs, or Bragg's Law is satisfied when the
vector $(\mathbf{s} - \mathbf{s}_0)/\lambda$ coincides with the reciprocal lattice vector $\mathbf{d}^*_{hkl}$ of the
reflecting planes.

The vector form of Bragg's Law may be combined with each of the three
Laue equations: i.e. for the first Laue equation:

$$\mathbf{a} \cdot (\mathbf{s} - \mathbf{s}_0) = n_x \lambda = \mathbf{a} \cdot \mathbf{d}^*_{hkl} \cdot \lambda = \mathbf{a} \cdot (h\mathbf{a}^* + k\mathbf{b}^* + l\mathbf{c}^*)\lambda.$$

Hence $n_x = h$ (since $\mathbf{a} \cdot \mathbf{a}^* = 1$, $\mathbf{a} \cdot \mathbf{b}^* = 0$, etc.), and similarly $n_y = k$ and $n_z = 1$
for the other Laue equations. The integers n_x, n_y and n_z of the Laue equations
are simply the Laue indices h, k, l of the reflecting planes.

Bragg's Law, like Newton's Laws, and all such uncomplicated expressions
in physics, is deceptively simple. Its applicability and relevance to problems
in X-ray and electron diffraction only unfold themselves gradually (to
teachers and students alike!). Newton was once asked how he made his great

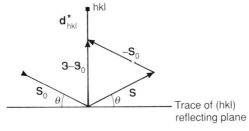

Fig. 7.7. Bragg's Law expressed in vector notation. Vectors $(\mathbf{s} - \mathbf{s}_0)$ and $\mathbf{d}^*_{hkl}$ are parallel and the
ratio of their moduli is λ. Hence Bragg's Law is expressed as $(\mathbf{s} - \mathbf{s}_0) = \mathbf{d}^*_{hkl}$.
$\quad\quad\quad\quad\quad\quad\quad\quad\quad\quad\quad\quad\quad\quad\quad\quad\quad\quad\quad\quad\quad\quad\quad\quad\quad\lambda$

discoveries: he replied 'by always thinking unto them'. The student of crystallography could do no better with respect to Bragg's Law!

7.5 Ewald's synthesis: the reflecting sphere construction

Ewald's synthesis is a geometrical formulation or expression of Bragg's Law which involves the reciprocal lattice and a 'sphere of reflection'. It is best illustrated and understood by way of an example. Consider a crystal with the (*hkl*) reflecting planes (Laue indices) at the correct Bragg angle (Fig. 7.8). The reciprocal lattice vector $\mathbf{d}^*_{hkl}$ is also shown. Now draw a sphere (the reflecting or Ewald sphere) of radius $1/\lambda$ (where λ is the X-ray wavelength) with the crystal at the centre. Since Bragg's Law is satisfied it may be shown that the Vector **0B** (from the point where the direct beam exits from the sphere to the point where the diffracted beam exits from the sphere) is identical to $\mathbf{d}^*_{hkl}$: i.e. from the triangle AOC, $|\mathbf{0C}| = 1/\lambda \sin\theta = 1/2|\mathbf{d}^*_{hkl}| = 1/2d_{hkl}$, i.e. $\lambda = 2d_{hkl} \sin\theta$. Hence, if the origin of the reciprocal lattice is shifted from the centre of the sphere (A) to the point where the direct beam exits from the sphere (0), then $\mathbf{0B} = \mathbf{d}^*_{hkl}$ and Bragg's Law is equivalent to the statement that the reciprocal lattice point for the reflecting planes (*hkl*) should intersect the sphere; the diffracted beam direction being given by the vector **AB**—i.e. the line from the centre of the sphere to the point where the reciprocal lattice point $\mathbf{d}^*_{hkl}$ intersects the sphere. Conversely, if the reciprocal lattice point does **not** intersect the sphere then Bragg's Law is not satisfied and no diffracted beams occur.

Figure 7.8 shows the construction of just one reflecting plane and one

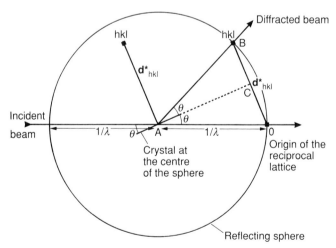

Fig. 7.8. The Ewald reflecting sphere construction for a set of planes at the correct Bragg angle. A sphere (the Ewald or reflecting sphere) is drawn, of radius $1/\lambda$ with the crystal at the centre. The vector **0B** is identical to $\mathbf{d}^*_{hkl}$. The origin of the reciprocal lattice is fixed at 0 and the reciprocal lattice point *hkl* intersects the sphere at the exit point of the diffracted beam.

reciprocal lattice point. It is a simple matter to extend it to all the reciprocal lattice points in a crystal. Figure 7.9(a) shows a section of the reciprocal lattice of a monoclinic crystal perpendicular to the **b*** reciprocal lattice vector [i.e. the *y*-axis—see Fig. 6.2(b)]. All the reciprocal lattice points in this section have indices of the form $h0l$. An incident X-ray beam is directed along the **a*** reciprocal lattice vector [i.e. along a direction in the crystal perpendicular to the *y*- and *z*-axes—see Fig. 6.2(a)]. The centre of the reflecting sphere is at a distance $1/\lambda$ from the origin of the reciprocal lattice along the line of the incident beam: note again that the origin of the reciprocal lattice is **not** at the centre of the sphere but is at the point where the direct beam exits from the sphere.

In the section shown, Fig. 7.9(a), the reflecting sphere intersects the 201 reciprocal lattice point: hence the only plane for which Bragg's Law is satisfied is the (201) plane and the direction of the 201 reflected beam is as indicated.

Figure 7.9(a) only shows one layer or section of the reciprocal lattice (through the origin) and a (diametral) section of the reflecting sphere. But the reciprocal lattice sections above and below the plane of the page need to be taken into account and also the smaller non-diametral sections of the reflecting sphere which intersects them. Figure 7.9(b) shows the 'next layer above' or $h1l$ section of the reciprocal lattice (see Fig. 6.3) and the smaller, non-diametral section of the reflecting sphere which it intersects. Notice that this section of the sphere does **not** pass through 010 (the reciprocal lattice point immediately 'above' the origin 000). The sphere intersects the $21\bar{1}$ reciprocal lattice point, hence the $(21\bar{1})$ plane also satisfies Bragg's Law and the direction of the $21\bar{1}$ reflected beam is from the centre of the sphere [which is **not** the point in the centre of this smaller circle but the point in the centre of the sphere in the reciprocal lattice section below—Fig. 7.9(a)] and the $21\bar{1}$ reciprocal lattice point. The reflected beam direction therefore cannot be drawn in Fig. 7.9(b) because it is directed upwards, out of the plane of the page.

Clearly, the construction can be extended to other reciprocal lattice sections, i.e. through the $h2l$, $h3l$, etc. sections (above); the $h\bar{1}l$, $h\bar{2}l$, $h\bar{3}l$, etc. sections (below) and so on. The further the reciprocal lattice section is from the origin, the smaller is the section of the reflecting sphere which it intersects. In the example above, the sphere only intersects the $h0l$, section [Fig. 7.9(a)], the $h1l$ section [Fig. 7.9(b)] and the $h\bar{1}l$ section (below), but no more. Hence only these sections, and the reciprocal lattice points within them, need to be considered.

In Fig. 7.9 the relative sizes of the reciprocal lattice and the sphere happen to be such that just one reciprocal lattice point in each section intersects the sphere. Clearly if the diameter of the sphere were made a little larger (i.e. the X-ray wavelength were made a little smaller) then no reciprocal lattice points would intersect the sphere and no planes in the crystal would be at the

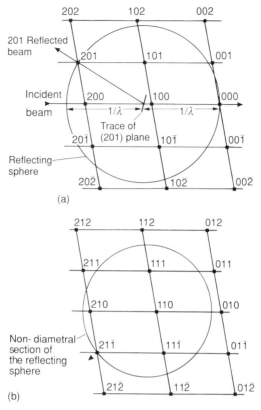

(a)

(b)

Fig. 7.9. The Ewald reflecting sphere construction for a monoclinic crystal in which the incident X-ray beam is directed along the **a*** reciprocal lattice vector. (a) Shows the *h0l* reciprocal lattice section [through the origin and perpendicular to the **b*** reciprocal lattice vector or *y*-axis see Fig. 6.2(c) and Fig. 6.3] and a diametral section of the reflecting sphere, radius $1/\lambda$. The 201 reciprocal lattice point intersects the sphere and the direction of the 201 reflected beam is indicated. (b) Shows the *h1l* reciprocal lattice section (i.e. the layer 'above' the *h0l* section) and the smaller, non-diametral section of the reflecting sphere. The $21\bar{1}$ reciprocal lattice point intersects the sphere, the direction of the $21\bar{1}$ reflected beam is 'upwards' from the centre of the sphere (in the *h0l* section below) through the $21\bar{1}$ reciprocal lattice point as indicated by the arrow-head.

correct Bragg angle for reflection; if the diameter of the sphere were continuously made larger (or smaller) than that shown in Fig. 7.9, then other planes would reflect as their reciprocal lattice points successively intersected the sphere. This is the basis of Laue's original X-ray experiment; 'white' X-radiation was used which contains a range of wavelengths, which correspond to a range or 'nest' of spheres of different diameters. Any plane whose reciprocal lattice point falls within this range will therefore satisfy Bragg's Law for one particular wavelength.

The situation is illustrated in Fig. 7.10, again for the *h0l* reciprocal lattice section of the monoclinic crystal shown in Fig. 7.9(a). The shaded region indicates a 'nest' of spheres with diameters in the wavelength range from largest wavelength (smallest sphere diameter) to smallest wavelength (largest sphere diameter). All the planes whose reciprocal lattice points lie within this region satisfy Bragg's Law for the particular sphere on which they lie.

The Laue technique is unique in that it utilizes white X-radiation. All the others utilize monochromatic or near-monochromatic (K_a) X-radiation. In order to obtain diffraction therefore, the crystal and the sphere (of a fixed diameter) must be moved relative to one another; whenever a reciprocal lattice point touches the sphere then 'out shoots' a diffracted (or reflected) beam from the centre of the sphere in a direction through the reciprocal lattice point. There are many ways in which these relative movements may be achieved in practice—the crystal may be rotated (rotation pattern), oscillated (oscillation pattern), precessed (precession pattern) or the crystal **and** the recording film may be oscillated (Weissenberg pattern). The details of these techniques lie beyond the scope of this handbook, but the basis of all of them—the Ewald reflecting sphere construction—is the same.

Fig. 7.10. The Ewald reflecting sphere construction for the $h0l$ reciprocal lattice section of the monoclinic crystal shown in Fig. 7.9(a) for the 'white' X-radiation, i.e. for a range of wavelengths from the smallest (largest sphere) to the largest (smallest sphere) giving rise to a 'nest' of spheres (shaded region) all passing through the origin. The 102, 201, 200 and 20$\bar{1}$ reciprocal lattice points lying within this region satisfy Bragg's Law, each for the particular wavelength or sphere which they intersect. The directions of the reflected beams from these planes are indicated by the arrows.

7.6 Applications of the reflecting sphere construction to electron diffraction

The wavelength associated with electrons depends on the accelerating voltage; for example in an electron microscope operated at 100 KV the wavelength is ~ 3.7 pm and at 1 MV it is ~ 0.8 pm. These wavelengths are very much smaller than the lattice parameters of crystals, which are normally in the range of 0.3 nm–3 nm. Hence the diameter of the reflecting sphere is very large in comparison with the size of the unit cell of the reciprocal lattice. Referring to the reciprocal lattice section in Fig. 7.9(a) as an example, the centre of the reflecting sphere would be situated along the direction of the incident beam at a point far to the left of the origin of the reciprocal lattice, well beyond the edge of the paper.

The situation for a simple cubic crystal is illustrated in Fig. 7.11 which shows that part of the reciprocal lattice section perpendicular to the $\mathbf{b}^*$ reciprocal lattice vector or y-axis (out of the plane of the paper) which lies close to the surface of the reflecting sphere. The incident electron beam is directed along the $\mathbf{a}^*$ reciprocal lattice vector or x-axis.

Close to the origin, 000, the curvature of the sphere is so small that it approximates to a plane perpendicular to the direction of the electron beam and hence passes (in this section) very close to the 001, 002, 003 and 00$\bar{1}$, 00$\bar{2}$, 00$\bar{3}$ reciprocal lattice points.

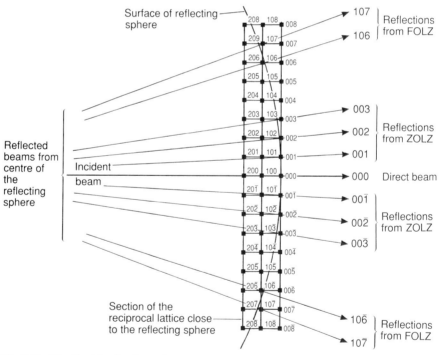

Fig. 7.11. The Ewald reflecting sphere construction for a simple cubic crystal in which the electron beam is incident along the $\mathbf{a}^*$ reciprocal lattice vector (x-axis). The $\mathbf{b}^*$ reciprocal lattice vector (y-axis) is perpendicular to the plane of the page. A section of the sphere (centre beyond the left hand edge of the page) and the reflected beams passing at small angles from the centre of the sphere through the reciprocal lattice points in the ZOLZ (giving spots close to the direct beam) and FOLZ (giving spots further away from the direct beam) are indicated.

In order for Bragg's Law to be satisfied exactly, the reciprocal lattice point must lie precisely on the reflecting sphere—but a diffracted beam will occur when the reciprocal lattice point is deviated a small (reciprocal) distance away from the sphere. This situation arises because reciprocal lattice points are not geometrical points but have a finite size—they are extended beyond their geometrical centres. A description of the amount and distribution of this extension is beyond the scope of this handbook, but some indication as to its origins can be given.

Firstly, the shape and size of reciprocal lattice points† are reciprocally related to the size and shape of the crystal. For example, the reciprocal lattice 'points' of a thin, plate-shaped crystal are rods or spikes orientated normally to the plane of the crystal—i.e. the small dimension of the plate corresponds to the large dimension of the rods or spikes. Secondly, distortion or bending of the lattice planes results in a corresponding extension of the reciprocal lattice points.

These conditions—small crystal size and distortion of the lattice planes—apply particularly to the thin foil specimens used in electron microscopy. Hence those reciprocal lattice points which lie in reciprocal lattice sections perpendicular, or nearly perpendicular, to the electron beam and which lie close to the Ewald reflecting sphere will give rise to diffracted beams.

Hence (referring again to Fig. 7.11), the reciprocal lattice points $001, 002,$ $003, 00\bar{1}, 00\bar{2}, 00\bar{3}$ which lie in a reciprocal lattice row perpendicular to the electron beam direction give rise to reflected beams, which are directed from the centre of the sphere (to the far left of the page) as indicated. Similar considerations apply to the reciprocal lattice row in the 'next layer above the page', i.e. the row through 010 (above 000), $011, 012, 013$, etc. and also the next layer below, i.e. through $0\bar{1}0$ (below 000) $0\bar{1}1, 0\bar{1}2, 0\bar{1}3$, etc. All of these reciprocal lattice points lie in the $(0kl)$ plane or section of the reciprocal lattice which is perpendicular to the electron beam direction. In summary, therefore, the reciprocal lattice points close to the origin, in the $(0kl)$ reciprocal lattice section perpendicular to the electron beam direction, give rise to reflected beams.

Since the diffraction angles are small (Fig. 7.11), the pattern of spots on the screen perpendicular to the beam corresponds to the pattern of reciprocal lattice points. Figure 7.12 shows this pattern of spots from the $(0kl)$ reciprocal lattice section grouped around the direct beam. For simplicity and clarity, only those reflected beams of type $00l$ (in the section perpendicular to the y-axis Fig. 7.11) are indexed.

These diffraction spots are said to belong to the zero-order Laue zone (ZOLZ for short) since they all arise from reciprocal lattice points in a

---

†Since reciprocal lattice 'points' have finite dimensions, depending upon the size and shape of the crystal, they may be described more precisely as **nodes**. However, the word **point** continues to be used, although it should be understood that reciprocal lattice points are geometrical points only for the case of infinitely large perfect crystals.

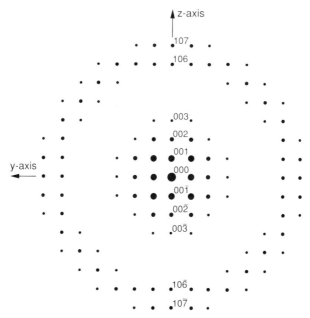

Fig. 7.12. The diffraction pattern on a screen perpendicular to the electron beam direction. The $0kl$ ZOLZ spots are grouped around the direct beam (centre spot) and the $1kl$ FOLZ spots are grouped roughly in a ring outside. Only the $h0l$ spots in the section perpendicular to the y-axis (Fig. 7.11) are indexed.

section through the origin or, equivalently, they all arise from planes in a zone: the zone axis being parallel (or nearly parallel) to the electron beam direction.

Referring again to Fig. 7.11, as we proceed along the surface of the reflecting sphere away from the origin, we begin to intersect the next row of reciprocal lattice points which does not pass through the origin. The reciprocal lattice points in this row which lie close to the sphere, i.e. 106, 107, $10\bar{6}$ and $10\bar{7}$ (and in the corresponding rows above and below the plane of the diagram, all of which lie in the $(1kl)$ section of the reciprocal lattice), will also give rise to diffraction spots as indicated. These spots, which lie outside those from the zero-order Laue zone away from the centre of the pattern (Fig. 7.12) are said to belong to the first-order Laue zone (FOLZ for short). Continuing outwards towards the edge of Fig. 7.11 we come to reciprocal lattice points in the second-order Laue zone (SOLZ for short). These are just the first two in a series of higher-order Laue zones (HOLZ for short).

The analysis of electron diffraction patterns is essentially a process of identifying the reciprocal lattice sections which give rise to them. Several computer programs are now available (see Appendix 2) which generate reciprocal lattice sections, given as input data the lattice parameters and type of unit cell and the electron beam (zone axis) direction. Several examples showing the ZOLZ only are given in Fig. 7.13. Care must be exercised in using such data because many different electron diffraction patterns from different types of crystals have identical symmetry and only differ in scale. For example the $\langle 111 \rangle_{\text{fcc}}$ and $[0001]_{\text{hcp}}$ patterns shown in Fig. 7.13(b) and (d) both consist of hexagonal patterns of points.

The first step in the analysis of electron diffraction patterns is measurement of the *d*-spacings. This is an easy matter. Figure 7.14 shows a set of reflecting planes at the Bragg angle θ (much exaggerated) to the electron beam. The diffracted beam, at angle $\theta + \theta = 2\theta$, to the direct beam, falls on the screen at a distance R from the centre spot. Figure 7.14 does not represent the **actual** ray paths in the electron microscope, which are of course determined and controlled by the lens settings: hence L, the camera length, is not the **actual** distance between the specimen and screen, but is a 'projected' distance which varies with the lens settings.

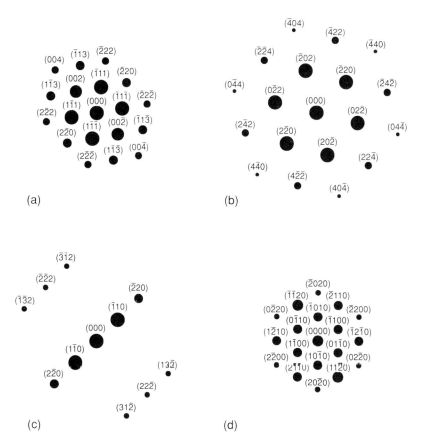

Fig. 7.13. Examples of the computer-generated diffraction patterns, drawn to the same scale ($\lambda L = 16.3$ Å mm). (a) Aluminium (fcc), zone axis $= \langle 110 \rangle$, (b) aluminium (fcc), zone axis $= \langle 111 \rangle$, (c) iron (bcc), zone axis $= \langle 112 \rangle$, (d) titanium (hcp), zone axis $= [0001]$.

Fig. 7.14. Idealized representation of the direct and diffracted ray paths in the electron microscope between the specimen and the screen. L is the camera length and R is the distance between the centre spot (direct beam) and diffracted spot.

From Fig. 7.14, $\tan 2\theta = R/L$. Since θ is small, $\tan 2\theta \approx 2\theta$. Similarly for Bragg's Law $\lambda = 2d_{hkl} \sin \theta \approx 2d_{hkl}\theta$. Eliminating θ from these equations we have:

$$d_{hkl} = \lambda L/R$$

where λL is known as the camera constant and which, like L, varies with lens settings in the microscope. The units of λL are best expressed in terms of the product of R, the distance measured on the screen (e.g. mm) and d_{hkl} (e.g. nm, Å or pm). Although the Ångstrom (Å) is not an SI (Systeme Internationale) unit, it is coherent with the SI system (1 Å = 10^{-10} m) and still remains in widespread use in crystallography (a) because it is roughly equal to atomic diameters and (b) because X-ray d-spacing data in the Powder Diffraction File prepared by the JCPDS (Joint Committee for Powder Diffraction Standards) and formerly known as the ASTM (American Society for Testing and Materials) Index is recorded in Ångstroms.

The accuracy with which the d-spacings can be measured is very limited because of the size or 'diffuseness' of the diffraction spots. Moreover the camera constant, λL, will only be known to a high degree of accuracy if a 'standard' specimen is used which gives a diffraction pattern with spots of accurately known d-spacings. Otherwise the small variations in lens settings from specimen to specimen and from day-to-day will limit the accuracy of λL

values at best to three significant figures. Hence, as pointed out above, patterns which have identical symmetry but which only differ slightly in scale with respect to the *d*-spacings of the diffraction spots are not readily distinguished.

The spots may then be indexed by reference to tables of data such as are contained in the Powder Diffraction File, which show the (Laue) indices, *hkl*, corresponding to the measured *d*-spacings. In doing so, a further step is required: the indexing must be such that the addition rule (Section 6.4.3, p. 75) is satisfied. A given set or family of planes {*hkl*} (which are invariably listed in data files simply as *hkl*—no brackets) will consist of a number of variants of identical *d*-spacings. For example, in the cubic system (see Section 5.4, p. 59) there are six variants of the 'plane of the form' {100}, all of which have identical *d*-spacings. The procedure consists of **choosing** the appropriate variants such that the addition rule is satisfied. Consider for example Fig. 7.13(a). The four spots of identical *d*-spacings closest to the centre spot are all reflections from planes of the form {111}. The particular indices have been chosen such that the indices of the remaining spots are determined correctly. For example $\mathbf{d}^*_{1\bar{1}1} + \mathbf{d}^*_{\bar{1}11} = \mathbf{d}^*_{002}$ and the zone axis, [110] is found by cross-multiplication of any pair of these indices (Section 6.4.5, p. 76). The 'choice' only needs to be made once, and having been made, all the other spots in the pattern can be indexed consistently by repeated application of the addition rule; again, with reference to Fig. 7.13(a), $\mathbf{d}^*_{1\bar{1}1} + \mathbf{d}^*_{002} = \mathbf{d}^*_{1\bar{1}3}$ and so on. The 'choice' is of course arbitrary: the number of different choices which can be made, all leading to a self-consistently indexed diffraction pattern, depends on the number of equivalent variants of the zone axis. In a cubic crystal there are 12 variants of the ⟨110⟩ direction, hence there are 12 ways in which a pattern like that of Fig. 7.13(a) can be indexed.

The availability of computer-generated diffraction patterns has greatly facilitated the indexing and verification of electron diffraction pattern analyses. However, it must be said that many 'useful' diffraction patterns—i.e. those which may be of potential scientific interest, which have been obtained under conditions of experimental difficulty and which may consist of many spots from several crystals of varying degrees of visibility on the film—still require for their solution careful observation and measurement and an awareness of the possible occurrence of additional complicating factors such as double diffraction. These topics are however the subject-matter of books and compendia on electron microscopy techniques, a number of which are listed under 'Further Reading' on p. 126.

7.7 The intensities of diffracted beams

The Laue equations and Bragg's Law have been derived on the basis that single atoms, of unspecified scattering power, are situated at each lattice point (Section 7.3). The analyses therefore provide no information about the intensities of the diffracted beams. This is a very large topic, beyond the scope of this handbook, but some indication of the factors which need to be taken into account, the quantities which are derived, and the problems associated with intensity measurements can be given for the case of X-ray diffraction.

Since it is the electrons in atoms which are primarily the scatterers of X-rays, the scattering amplitude of an electron, and the variation in the scattering amplitude with angle, is first determined. Then the scattering amplitude of an atom is determined by summing the contributions from all Z electrons (where $Z =$ the atomic number)—the summation taking into account the path or phase differences between all the Z scattered waves. The result of this analysis is expressed by a dimensionless number, f, the *atomic scattering factor*, which is the ratio of the scattering amplitude of the atom to that of a single (classical) electron. At zero scattering angle, where all the scattered waves are in phase, $f = Z$; as the scattering angle increases, f falls below Z because of the increasingly destructive interference effects between the Z scattered waves.

The scattering amplitude of a unit cell is determined by summing the scattering amplitudes f, from all the atoms in the unit cell (equivalent to all the atoms in the motif in the case of a primitive unit cell). Again, the summation must take into account the path or phase differences between all the scattered waves and is again expressed as a (dimensionless) number called F_{hkl}, the structure factor. F_{hkl} must not only express the amplitude of scattering from an (hkl) reflecting plane, but it must also express the phase angle of the scattered wave. F_{hkl} therefore is represented as a vector, or algebraically as a complex number.

Crystal structure determination is a two-part process: (a) the determination of the size and shape of the unit cell (i.e. the lattice parameters) from the geometry of the diffraction pattern and (b) the determination of the lattice type and distribution of the atoms in the structure, from the (relative) intensities of the diffraction spots. Part (a) is in principle a straightforward process; (b) is not, because films and counters record intensities which are proportional to the **squares** of the amplitudes. The square of a complex number, F_{hkl}, is always real and hence the information about the phase angles of the diffracted beams is lost. A major problem in crystal structure determination is, in effect, the recovery of this phase information and requires for its solution as much insight and intuition as mathematical and crystallographic knowledge. A graphic account of the problems involved in the epoch-making determination of the structure of DNA is given by one of those most closely involved, J. D. Watson, in his book *The Double Helix*.

The distinction between the direction-problem and intensity-problem of diffracted beams from crystals has its corollary in the diffraction of light from diffraction gratings. A (primitive) crystal with one atom per lattice point may be regarded as being analogous to a 'narrow slit' diffraction grating in which each slit can be regarded as the source of a single Huygens' wavelet which propagates uniformly in all directions (Fig. 7.2). Only the interference effects of light emanating from different slits (equivalent to single atoms at lattice points) need to be taken into account and these determine the directions of the diffracted beams (Section 7.2). The intensities of the diffracted beams are proportional to the squares of the scattered amplitudes of the Huygens' wavelets (for light) or the atomic scattering factor of the single atoms (for X-rays).

A (primitive) crystal with a motif consisting of more than one atom, may be regarded as being analogous to a 'wide slit' diffraction grating in which the interference effects from all the Huygens' wavelets distributed **across** each slit also need to be taken into account. These interference effects determine the intensities of the diffracted beams, but not their directions. The diffraction pattern from a wide-slit diffraction grating may be expressed as that from a narrow-slit grating in which the intensities of the diffracted beams are modulated by the intensity distribution predicted to occur from a single wide slit. In the case of X-ray diffraction from crystals it is the structure factor which expresses the interference effects from all the atoms in the unit cell and which modulates, in effect, the intensities of the diffracted beams. The analogy may be pressed a little further: in the diffraction of light, missing orders may occur in which complete destructive interference occurs in a particular diffraction direction from a single wide slit; in the diffraction of X-rays (and electrons) forbidden reflections may occur depending upon the lattice type and the symmetry elements present.

Hence, to conclude, it is the dimensions of the repeating unit—the lattice parameters of a crystal or the line spacing in a grating—which determine the directions of the diffracted beams and the geometry of the pattern; and it is the interference effects from the atoms in the unit cell and the lattice type, or from a single slit in a grating, which determine the intensities of the diffracted beams.

Exercises

1. Iron [bcc, $a = 0.2866$ nm (2.866 Å)] is irradiated with $CrK\alpha$ X-radiation [$\lambda = 0.2291$ nm (2.291 Å)]. Find the indices $\{hkl\}$ and d-spacings of the planes which give rise to X-ray reflections.
   Note: In body-centred lattices, reflection from planes for which $(h + k + l)$ does **not** equal an even integer are forbidden.
   Hint: Prepare a table listing the indices and d-spacings of the allowed reflecting planes in order of decreasing d-spacing and determine the θ angles for reflection using Bragg's Law.

2. Figure 7.15 is an electron diffraction pattern of a thin crystal of aluminium [fcc, $a = 0.4049$ nm (4.049 Å)] taken using an electron microscope operating at 100 kV, and shows diffraction spots from the ZOLZ (zero-order Laue zone) only.

Fig. 7.15. An electron diffraction pattern (ZOLZ) of a fcc crystal. The camera length L (adjusted for the print size) is 524 mm. (See Exercise 2.)

Given the electron wavelength $\lambda = 0.0037$ nm and the camera length $L = 524$ mm, index the diffraction spots and determine the zone axis of the diffraction pattern.

Note: In face-centred lattices, reflections from planes for which h, k and l are **not** all odd or all even integers are forbidden.

Hint: Prepare a table listing the indices $\{hkl\}$ and d-spacings of the allowed reflecting planes as for Exercise 1. Determine the d-spacings of the diffraction spots in the pattern (see Section 7.6) and hence, using the table, find their indices $\{hkl\}$. Using the addition rule in Section 6.4.3 (p. 75), assign a consistent set of indices hkl to the diffraction spots and hence find their common zone axis using the equation in Section 6.4.5 (p. 76). Check your answer by using one of the computer programs listed in Appendix 2.

3. In a Laue experiment, a bcc crystal, lattice parameter $a = 0.4$ nm (4 Å) is irradiated in the [100] (or $\mathbf{a}^*$) direction with an X-ray beam which contains a continuous spectrum of wavelengths in the range between 0.167 nm (1.67 Å) and 0.25 nm (2.5 Å). Use the reflecting sphere construction to determine the indices of the planes in the crystal for which Bragg's Law is satisfied and draw the direction of the reflected beam for **one** plane in the [001] zone.

Hint: Make a scale drawing of the section of the reciprocal lattice normal to the [001] (or $\mathbf{z}^*$) direction and which passes through the origin 000 [i.e. the section which contains the $hk0$ reciprocal lattice points as shown in Fig. 6.4(b)]. A convenient scale to use between the reciprocal lattice dimensions and A4 size drawing paper is $1 \text{ nm}^{-1} = 0.5$ cm ($1\text{Å}^{-1} = 5.0$ cm). Draw a line indicating the [100] direction of the incident beam and draw in the two reflecting spheres representing the limits of the wavelength range. Remember that the origin of the reciprocal lattice is located at the point where the beam **exits** from the spheres— hence the centres of the spheres are obviously not coincident. Shade in the region of the reciprocal lattice between the two spheres: planes whose reciprocal lattice points lie in this region satisfy Bragg's Law. For one reciprocal lattice point in this region, find, by construction, the sphere which it intersects. The direction of the reflected beam is from the centre of this sphere through the reciprocal lattice point, and the radius of the sphere gives the particular wavelength reflected.

Draw sections of the reciprocal lattice normal to the [001] (or z^*) direction and which pass through the $hk1$, $hk2$, $hk\bar{1}$, $hk\bar{2}$, etc. reciprocal lattice points (see Fig. 6.5). In these sections of the reciprocal lattice 'above' and 'below' that through the origin, the sections of the sphere are reducing in size—simple trigonometry will show by how much. Again, planes whose reciprocal lattice points lie in the region between the spheres satisfy Bragg's Law.

4. In an oscillating crystal experiment the bcc crystal described in Exercise 3 is irradiated in the [100] (or a^*) direction with a monochromatic X-ray beam of wavelength 0.167 nm (1.67 Å). The crystal is then oscillated $\pm 10°$ about the [001] (or z^*) direction. Find the indices $hk0$ of the planes in the [001] zone which give rise to reflections during the oscillation of the crystal.

   Hint: Make a scale drawing of the section of the reciprocal lattice through the origin 000 and normal to the [001] (or z^*) direction. Draw a line indicating the [100] direction of the incident beam and a single sphere corresponding to the single X-ray wavelent (see Exercise 3). Oscillating the crystal (at the centre of the sphere) is equivalent to oscillating the reciprocal lattice (at the origin). The simplest way to represent the relative changes in orientation between the crystal and the X-ray beam is to 'oscillate' the beam. The directions of the beam at the oscillation limits are $\pm 10°$ from the [100] direction in the plane of the reciprocal lattice section. Draw in the reflecting sphere at these limits and shade in the regions of reciprocal space through which the surface of the sphere passes. Planes whose reciprocal lattice points lie in these regions reflect the X-ray beam during oscillation.

5. In an electron diffraction experiment the bcc crystal described in Exercises 3 and 4 is irradiated in the [001] (or a^*) direction with an electron beam of wavelength 0.002 nm (0.02 Å). Find the reciprocal lattice points which lie close to the sphere in the ZOLZ (zero-order Laue zone) and FOLZ (first-order Laue zone).

   Hint: Using the same reciprocal lattice scale as in Exercise 3 and 4, it will be found that a very large sheet of paper and very large compasses are needed to draw the complete reflecting sphere! However, a sketch of the surface of the sphere near the origin will suffice. In electron diffraction, sections of the reciprocal lattice perpendicular to the electron beam (i.e. normal to the [100] or a^*) direction are most convenient. Draw the section through the origin 000 containing the $0kl$ reciprocal lattice points (i.e. the ZOLZ), and the section containing the $1kl$ reciprocal lattice points (i.e. the FOLZ) (see also Fig. 6.5). Estimate the regions of these reciprocal lattice sections, and hence the reciprocal lattice points, which are close to the surface of the reflecting sphere.

Appendix 1: Useful components for a crystallography model-building kit and suppliers

The crystal models may be made from expanded polystyrene or solid plastic balls. A range of sizes is available and the cost increases roughly in proportion to the cube of the diameter. Unfortunately, it is not possible to select balls with diameter ratios $1:0.732:0.414:0.225:0.291$ (i.e. the useful diameter ratios for interstitial sites) and it is simplest to make interstitial atoms out of Plasticine.

Griffin and George Ltd., Bishop Meadow Road, Loughborough LE11 0RG (Tel. 0509-233344). Markets expanded polystyrene 'Grifzote' spheres in sizes from 12.5 to 51 mm diameter. They may be glued together with Bostik or linked together with wire rods to make expanded models. Jigs are available for making holes in different configurations in the spheres for inserting the rods.

The Precision Plastic Ball Company, 12 Green Lane, Addingham LS29 0JH (Tel. 0943-831166). Markets a range of solid plastic balls some in different colours and sizes from 3 mm to 3 inches. Materials include polypropene, acrylic, and polystyrene. The 1-inch or $\frac{1}{2}$-inch sizes are probably most useful. Superglue gives a quick and effective bond.

Your local grocery shop sells sugar-cubes from which cubic crystal models showing different point symmetries may be made. (The author has not found an alternative source of inexpensive cubes; children's modelling bricks are usually orthorhombic.) Woodworkers' water-based resin gives a satisfactory bond; saturated sugar solution is slow and rather ineffective.

Gallenkamp, 27 Yarm Road, Stockton-on-Tees TS18 3NJ (Tel. 0642-673441). Markets molecular model kits based on 22 mm diameter plastic balls available in different colours, drilled with a range of hole configurations and which can be linked by springs of different lengths. These can be used to build 'expanded' models of crystal structures. Perhaps the most useful balls are those drilled with a 'universal' hole configuration which may be used for most symmetries and co-ordinations.

Beevers Miniature Models, Edinburgh University, West Mains Road, Edinburgh EH9 3JJ (Tel. 031-667-1081). Markets molecular model kits based on 6.9 and 4.9 mm diameter balls, available in different colours and drilled with a range of hole configurations, and which can be linked with wire rods. Complete models of a wide range of crystal structures are also available.

Cochranes of Oxford Ltd., Leafield, Oxford OX8 5NY (Tel. 099387-641). Markets molecular model kits based on plastic atom centres joined by short plastic tubes. The centres are moulded in a variety of shapes, and are colour coded according to the element. The kits can be used to build a range of molecules and extended lattices. Complete models of a wide range of crystal structures are also available.

Appendix 2: Computer programs in crystallography

Atom Packing and Crystal Structure by K. M. Crennell and L. S. Dent Glasser. Sophisticated 3-D graphics make the stacking of atoms extremely clear (also for Archimedes).

3-D Viewing of Polymeric and Small Molecules by C. M. Warwick and T. W. Clyne.
Provides a tool for the study of the three-dimensional shapes of molecules.

Point and Space Groups by J. M. Hyde, M. J. Goringe, J. P. Jakubovics and G. D. W. Smith.
Permits the student's understanding of symmetry and space groups to be explored.

The Stereographic Projection by J. M. Towner.
Presents structured questions on the application of the stereogram and their answers.

Electron Diffraction by P. J. Goodhew.
Examines various aspects of electron scattering and diffraction as they are encountered in courses in electron microscopy.

The above five programs are marketed by **The Institute of Materials** (1 Carlton House Terrace, London SW1Y 5DB)—part of a range of refereed and tested computer software packages available on disc for the IBM PC and Acorn Micros.

Alchemy II: Molecular Modelling
For the IBM PC XT/AT, PS/2 or compatible and Mac II.
From Tripos Associates, Centennial Court, Easthampstead Road, Bracknell, Berks RG12 1NN.

Atoms: Atomic Structure Display Software
Includes molecules, polymers and an optional library of silicate structures. For the IBM PC XT/AT, PS/2 and clones, and Mac.
From Shape Software, 521 Hidden Valley Road, Kingsport, TN 37663, USA.

Ball and Stick
A 3-D molecular graphics package designed for the Apple Mac, uses pull down menus and mouse.
From Cherwell Scientific Publishing, The Magdalen Centre, Oxford Science Park, Oxford OX4 4GA.

Crystals
A complete X-ray crystallography package developed on a VAX and now runs on an IBM PC. Details from Dr D. Watkin, Department of Chemical Crystallography, University of Oxford, OX1 3PD.

Crystal Structure and Lattice Energy
An introductory program, for secondary school and A-level standard, for BBC Micros and RM 380Z and 480Z computers. From the Science Education Group, University of York, York YO1 5DD.

Diffract and Diffract Version 1.3
A very comprehensive program which includes the following sub-programs: diffraction patterns, HOLZ patterns, stereographic projections, Kikuchi lines and the real lattice and five utility programs which determine specific numerical values in crystals, namely d-spacings, angles between planes, angles between directions and a calculation dialogue box which provides useful quantities concerned with specific planes. Diffract Version 1.3 is an extended version of Diffract. For the Apple-Macintosh PC. From microdev Software 3120 NW John Olsen Avenue #D-104, Hillsboro, OR 97124, USA.

Difpat
A program that lists reciprocal lattice sections, in terms of the three shortest vectors, their ratios and interplanar angles. Available from Dr P. E. Champness, Department of Geology, The University of Manchester, Manchester M13 9PL. For Apple-Macintosh or IBM PCs.

Metal and Ionic
Two programs which introduce, at an elementary level, the three crystal structures and unit cell types relating to metals and the structural features of three compounds using space filling and ball and spoke images. For the various models of the BBC PC, Archimedes RM Nimbus and Master Compact. From AVP, School Hill Centre, Chepstow, NP6 5PH.

Planedir
A program for Miller indices, one of the range of crystallography programs for use on any IBM compatible computer. From Software Scientific Services, 3497 School Road, Murrysville, PA 15668, USA, for use on any IBM compatible computer.

Stereo
Plots 20 cm dia. stereographic projections of plane normals or zone directions. For the Apple-Macintosh PC. From Dr P. E. Champness, as above.

Appendix 3: Biographical notes on crystallographers mentioned in the text

William Barlow 1845–1934

Following an inheritance from his father, Barlow, one of the last great English amateurs in science, took up the study of crystallography in his early thirties and attempted to relate the properties of crystals to the packing arrangements of their constituent atoms. He collaborated with W. J. Pope at Cambridge and guessed (correctly) the structure of the alkali halides. His mathematical ability and developing interest in symmetry enabled him to extend the methods of Bravais and Sohncke to find the 'symmetrical groupings to fit the forms and compositions of a variety of different substances' but he did not publish his derivation of the 230 space groups until 1894, three years after Fedorov and Schoenflies, of whose work he almost certainly had no prior knowledge.

William Henry Bragg 1862–1942

W. H. Bragg read mathematics at Cambridge and was appointed Professor of Mathematics and Physics at Adelaide in 1885. For his first eighteen years there he published very little, but in 1903 became involved in problems of radiation, the ionization of gases and the nature of X-rays, which he considered to be 'material' in nature. His increasing reputation led to his appointment in 1908 as Cavendish Professor of Physics in the University of Leeds. In late 1912 he and his son, William Lawrence, became convinced that the Laue experiment made a wave hypothesis for X-rays unavoidable and together they made remarkably rapid advances in crystal structure analysis, the father's main contribution being the construction of an ionization chamber and crystal spectrometer and the solution of the structure of diamond. The work was interrupted by the First World War and, in 1915, Bragg moved from Leeds to University College, London, and then, in 1923, to the Royal Institution, at which places he laid one of the foundations of molecular biology by establishing research groups directed towards the analysis of organic crystals.

William Lawrence Bragg 1890–1971

W. L. Bragg obtained a degree in mathematics at the University of Adelaide and, on the return of the family to England, entered Trinity College, Cambridge, to study physics at the Cavendish Laboratory under Sir J. J. Thomson. In 1911 he obtained a lectureship at Trinity College. At that time he supported his father's view that X-rays had the 'properties of material particles rather than those of electromagnetic waves' but during the summer and autumn of 1912 both he and his father abandoned it in the light of Laue's discovery of X-ray diffraction. It is not known how the Braggs became acquainted with Laue's discovery; this may have been through the 250th anniversary meeting of The Royal Society in July 1912 or, somewhat later, a lecture by J. J. Thomson to the Leeds (or Manchester?) Physics Groups. The theory (of Stokes) that X-rays were very short pulses of electromagnetic radiation also gave rise to the notion of Bragg's mind that the pulses should be reflected 'by the sheets of atoms in the crystal as if these sheets were mirrors'—a profoundly simple notion that not only explained the shapes of the diffraction spots but also provided a simple geometrical basis for the analysis of crystal structures. This work progressed extremely rapidly. Bragg's study of Laue's diffraction patterns of ZnS (zinc blende) led to the (correct) postulate that the structure was based on an fcc lattice and in the winter of 1912–13 he had prepared and analysed his own 'Laue' photographs of NaCl and KCl. In collaboration with his father in the summer of 1913, and with the aid of the X-ray spectrometer, Bragg solved the structures of fluorspar (CaF_2), zinc blende (ZnS), iron pyrites (FeS_2), sodium nitrate ($NaNO_3$) and calcite ($CaCO_3$). The remainder (if it can be called that) of Bragg's scientific career saw the inexorable development of the techniques of X-ray (and electron) diffraction and the solution of the structures of crystals—particularly mineral and organic crystals—of greater and greater complexity. It was a development in which Bragg himself, as Langworthy Professor of Physics at the University of Manchester, as Cavendish Professor at Cambridge, and towards the end of his life, as Director of the Royal Institution, played no small part.

Auguste Bravais 1811–63

Bravais was born in Annonay in France, studied mathematics in Paris and became a naval cadet in Toulon, which enabled him to participate in explorations to Algeria and the North Cape. He was appointed Professor of Physics at the École Polytechnique in 1845, and his interest in the relationships between the external forms and internal structures of crystals led to the derivation of the fourteen space lattices in 1848—work which was partly based on Frankenheim's fifteen 'nodal' lattice types. However, constant application to a wide range of studies which aroused his curiosity led, in 1857, to a breakdown of his health, resignation from his post and retirement from the Navy.

Peter Paul Ewald 1890–1985

Ewald deserves greater recognition for his contribution to the interpretation of X-ray diffraction patterns than he has hitherto been accorded—unlike Laue or the Braggs he was not awarded a Nobel Prize. Yet his doctor's thesis of 1912 which he discussed with Laue, contained within it the bases of the 'reciprocal lattice and reflecting sphere construction' analyses of the geometry of (X-ray) diffraction which is equivalent to Bragg's Law. Indeed, it was only after reading Laue, Friedrich and Knipping's published papers that Ewald realized the relevance of his own approach and, in particular, the applicability of a formula in his thesis which he had brought to the attention of Laue but which in fact he (Laue) had not used.

Evgraph Stepanovich von Fedorov 1853–1919

Son of an army engineer, Fedorov attended military school in Kiev and became, in turn, a combat officer and member of the revolutionary underground. His first ideas on the derivation of the 230 space groups were contained in his book *The Elements of Configurations*, started in 1879, when he was 26 years old but not published until 1885. His complete derivation of the space groups was circulated in 1890 to his friends (including Schoenflies) as a series of preprints but was not published until 1891, shortly before Schoenflies' independent derivation.

Moritz Ludwig Frankenheim 1801–69

Frankenheim was born and educated in Brunswick and the University of Berlin, where he was appointed lecturer in 1826. He was subsequently appointed Professor of Physics at Breslau, a post which he held until 1866. It was in a work of 1835 that he showed there could only be fifteen 'nodal', i.e. space lattice types, which much later (1856) he corrected to fourteen configurations, 8 years after Bravais' derivation of the fourteen space lattices.

René-Just Haüy 1743–1822

The son of a poor weaver, Haüy received a classical and theological education at the College de Navarre in Paris and was ordained in 1770. His *Essai d'une théorie sur la structure des cristaux* of 1784 laid the foundation for the mathematical theory of crystal structure. In 1793 he proposed that there were six 'primary forms'—a parallelpiped, rhombic dodecahedron, hexagonal dipyramid, right hexagonal prism, octahedron and tetrahedron. In the *Traité de Minéralogie* of 1801, these were further divided which led to the notion of 'molécules intégrantes'. Haüy survived the Revolution and was made Honorary Canon of Notre Dame in 1802.

Appendix 3 109

Carl Heinrich Hermann 1898–1961

Formal structure theory, following the derivation of the 230 space groups by Fedorov, Schoenflies and Barlow, remained dormant even in the early years of crystal structure analyses by X-rays, largely because of the inconvenient and difficult notation then used. Hermann's great contribution (carried out initially independently of Mauguin) was to simplify the notation for the symmetry elements and space groups, making the theory much more accessible. Hermann was also instrumental in the preparation of the *Strukterberichte* (*Structure Reports*) from 1925–37. He was a member of the Society of Friends and after the Second World War (during which he was jailed for listening to BBC broadcasts) he was appointed Professor of Crystallography at Marburg, a post he held until his death.

Johann Friedrich Christian Hessel 1796–1872

Hessel was born and educated at Nuremberg but spent the most of his professional life as Professor of Mineralogy and Mining Technology at Marburg. He was the first to show (in 1830) that only two-, three-, four- and six-fold axes of symmetry can occur in crystals and that considerations of symmetry lead to the thirty-two crystal classes. However, his work was unrecognized by his contemporaries and remained so until long after his death.

Robert Hooke 1635–1703

Hooke attracted the attention of Robert Boyle at Oxford and it was through his mechanical skill that he made a success of Boyle's air pump. He became a Fellow of the Royal Society and held the post of 'Curator of Experiments' from 1662 until the end of his life. It was in this capacity that Hooke was solicited by the Council of the Royal Society to prosecute his microscopical observations in order to publish them and was also charged to bring in at every meeting one microscopical observation at least. Hooke more then fulfilled this onerous obligation and, in doing so, caused the great capability of the microscope to be realized in England. The fruit of his work, *Micrographia, or Some Physiological Descriptions of Minute Bodies made by Magnifying Glasses, with Observations and Inquiries Thereupon*', was printed in 1665. In this book the word 'cell', so important in biology, was first applied to describe the porous structure of cork.

Max von Laue 1879–1960

Laue was educated at the University of Berlin and became an assistant to (and favourite disciple of) Max Planck. He joined Sommerfeld's Theoretical

Physics Group at the University of Munich in 1909. His intuition—that the regular arrangement of atoms in a crystal might give rise to an interference effect if the waves travelling through were of a wavelength of the same order as the atom or 'resonator' spacing—almost certainly stems from a meeting with P. P. Ewald in January 1912. Ewald was completing his doctoral thesis and wished to discuss with Laue some of his conclusions. Laue encountered strong disbelief amongst his colleagues of any significant outcome of such a diffraction experiment on the grounds that the thermal motion of the atoms would obscure any diffraction maxima. However, he persevered and, with the assistance of Walter Friedrich (an assistant of Sommerfeld), and Paul Knipping (who had just finished his thesis under Roentgen), the famous experiment on a copper sulphate crystal which 'happened to be in the laboratory' was carried out. Laue's interpretation of the results was based upon the notion that the crystal behaves as a 'three-dimensional' diffraction grating but was also confused by a misapprehension that the wavelengths of the (diffracted) beams were those of characteristic or fluorescence X-rays in a crystal—a property of the atoms rather than the lattice.

Charles Mauguin 1878–1958

Mauguin's early career expectation was that of a teacher in a teacher's training college, but he quickly developed an interest in mathematics and natural philosophy and commenced his scientific work in the field of organic chemistry. His interest in crystallography probably stems from a course of lectures given by Pierre Curie which he attended in 1905. Mauguin was one of a small group of crystallographers who, in 1933, undertook the publication of the International Tables, and it is his symbolism of the 230 space groups (worked out in collaboration with C. H. Hermann) which is now in almost universal use.

William Hallowes Miller 1801–1880

Miller was educated at St. John's College, Cambridge where, in 1829, he became a Fellow. In 1839 he published *A Treatise on Crystallography*, in which he made the fundamental assertion that crystallographic reference axes should be parallel to possible crystal edges. His system of indexing was based on a 'parametral' plane making intercepts *a*, *b* and *c* on such axes [i.e. (111)]; a plane making intercepts *a/h*, *b/k* and *c/l* was assigned the (integral) indices (*hkl*). Although the algebraic advantages of this system were immediately apparent to his contemporaries (and were quickly adopted), their full significance was not fully appreciated until Bragg's and Ewald's interpretation of X-ray diffraction.

Louis Pasteur 1822–95

Pasteur is perhaps best remembered for his work in microbiology and immunology and, in particular, the practical applications—the discovery of vaccines, the treatments for rabies and anthrax, silkworm disease, etc. His work in crystallography was confined to the early years of his scientific career. Beginning in about 1847 (shortly after completing his dissertation in physics), he began a series of investigations into the relations between optical activity, crystalline structure and chemical composition in organic compounds. His guiding principle was that optical activity was somehow associated with life. Pasteur's demonstration that the optically inactive paratartaric (or racemic) acid was composed of equal amounts of two optically active forms of opposite senses was made on crystals of sodium–ammonium paratartrate. In using these, and in separating out the two forms, he was perhaps fortunate, as in no other compounds is the relationship between crystal structure and molecular asymmetry so straightforward; also, the distinctive 'hemihedral' crystalline forms of these compounds occur only under certain conditions of crystallization. From this he was led to study asparagine and its derivatives (aspartic acid and the aspartates, malic acid and the malates).

William Jackson Pope 1870–1939

Pope's major scientific work was in the field of organic chemistry. He was educated at Finsbury Technical College and the City and Guilds of London Institute in Kensington; in 1908 he was appointed Professor of Chemistry at Cambridge at the early age of 38. His crystallographic work extends over the period 1906–10 when, in collaboration with W. Barlow, he developed models of crystal structures based on the close-packing of ions or atoms of different sizes—models which were to prove so valuable to the Braggs in their analyses of crystal structures.

Arthur Schoenflies 1853–1928

Schoenflies was born in Landsberg an der Warte, now in Poland. He studied mathematics at Berlin and became successively high school teacher, Associate Professor of Mathematics (at Göttingen), Professor (at Königsberg) and Rector of the University at Frankfurt. He extended the work of Sohncke on periodic discrete groups by taking into consideration rotation–reflection and inversion axes of symmetry, adding another 165 to Sohncke's sixty-five groups. The work was completed in his book *Kristallsysteme und Kristallstruktur*, published in Leipzig in 1891, a few months after Fedorov's paper.

Leonhard Sohncke 1842–97

Sohncke was born in Halle, Germany, where his father was Professor of Mathematics at the University. Like his father he followed an academic career, being appointed to a succession of professorships in physics, firstly at Halle and at the end of his career at the Technische Hochschule in Munich. Sohncke considered the possible arrays of points which have identical environments but not necessarily in the same orientation (as in the definition of Bravais lattices), and arrived at sixty-five of the possible 230 space groups. He published his findings in 1879, while he was professor of Physics at the Technische Hochschule in Karlsruhe, and used cigar-box models by way of illustrations!

Gustav Heinrich Johann Apollon Tammann 1861–1938

Tammann can be regarded as a pioneer physical metallurgist in the light of his work in metallography and the study of solid-state chemical reactions. He was born in Yamburg (now Kingisepp) in Russia and, after a career as a lecturer at Charlottenburg and Leipzig, was chosen to head the newly formed Institute at Göttingen in 1903. It was here that he began his studies on metallic compounds, the crystal structures and mechanical properties of metals and alloys, and the general problems of the mechanisms of plastic deformation and work hardening in terms of crystallographic slip and crystalline rearrangements. He continued to work on these problems until shortly before his death, applying his ideas at the same time to the flow of ice.

Wilhelm Eduard Weber 1804–91

Weber was Professor of Physics at Göttingen from 1831 for most of his professional life and worked in collaboration with Gauss on magnetic phenomena. His main achievements were the introduction of a logical system of units for electricity, related to the fundamental units of mass, length and time and also the connection between electromagnetic phenomena and the velocity of light—a connection which was later thoroughly worked out by Maxwell. Weber was also one of the 'Göttingen Seven' who, in 1837, lost their university posts because of their opposition to the autocracy of King Ernst August of Hanover.

Christian Samuel Weiss 1780–1856

After studying medicine at Leipzig, Weiss switched to chemistry and physics, becoming Professor of Physics there in 1808. In 1810 he was appointed Professor of Physics at the newly established and prestigious University of

Berlin, a post which he held until his death. Weiss developed the idea of crystal axes, from which he was able to distinguish crystal systems by the ways in which crystal faces were related to such axes. He also formulated the concept of a zone: originally conceived as a direction of prominent crystal growth, the term was defined as a collection of crystal faces parallel to a line— the zone axis; from this concept the zone law was derived.

Appendix 4: Some useful geometrical relationships

In A4.1–A4.3 the rather lengthy expressions for the triclinic system are omitted.

A4.1 Interplanar spacings, d_{hkl}

Orthorhombic:

$$\frac{1}{d^2} = \frac{h^2}{a^2} + \frac{k^2}{b^2} + \frac{l^2}{c^2}.$$

(Tetragonal: $a = b$; cubic: $a = b = c$.)

Hexagonal:

$$\frac{1}{d^2} = \frac{4}{3}\left(\frac{h^2 + hk + k^2}{a}\right) + \frac{l^2}{c^2}.$$

Rhombohedral:

$$\frac{1}{d^2} = \frac{(h^2 + k^2 + l^2)\sin^2\alpha + 2(hk + kl + hl)(\cos^2\alpha - \cos\alpha)}{a^2(1 - 3\cos^2\alpha + 2\cos^3\alpha)}.$$

Monoclinic:

$$\frac{1}{d^2} = \frac{1}{\sin^2\beta}\left(\frac{h^2}{a^2} + \frac{k^2\sin^2\beta}{b^2} + \frac{l^2}{c^2} - \frac{2hl\cos\beta}{ac}\right).$$

A4.2 Interplanar angles, ρ, between planes $(h_1 k_1 l_1)$ and $(h_2 k_2 l_2)$

Orthorhombic:

$$\cos\rho = \frac{(h_1 h_2/a^2) + (k_1 k_2/b^2) + (l_1 l_2/c^2)}{\sqrt{\{[(h_1^2/a^2) + (k_1^2/b^2) + (l_1^2/c^2)][(h_2^2/a^2) + (k_2^2/b^2) + (l_2^2/c^2)]\}}}.$$

(tetragonal: $a = b$; cubic: $a = b = c$.)

114

Hexagonal:

$$\cos\rho = \frac{h_1 h_2 + k_1 k_2 + \frac{1}{2}(h_1 k_2 + h_2 k_1) + (3a^2/4c^2)l_1 l_2}{\sqrt{\{[h_1^2 + k_1^2 + h_1 k_1 + (3a^2/4c^2)l_1^2][h_2^2 + k_2^2 + h_2 k_2 + (3a^2/4c^2)l_2^2]\}}}.$$

Rhombohedral:

$$\begin{aligned}\cos\rho = (a^4 d_1 d_2/V^2)\,[&\sin^2\alpha(h_1 h_2 + k_1 k_2 + l_1 l_2)\\ &+ (\cos^2\alpha - \cos\alpha)(k_1 l_2 + k_2 l_1 + l_1 h_2 + l_2 h_1 + h_1 k_2 + h_2 k_1)].\end{aligned}$$

Monoclinic:

$$\cos\rho = \frac{d_1 d^2}{\sin^2\beta}\left[\frac{h_1 h_2}{a^2} + \frac{k_1 k_2 \sin^2\beta}{b^2} + \frac{l_1 l_2}{c^2} - \frac{(l_1 h_2 + l_2 h_1)\cos\beta}{ac}\right].$$

A4.3 Volumes of unit cells

Orthorhombic:

$$V = abc.$$

(Tetragonal: $a = b$; cubic: $a = b = c$.)

Hexagonal:

$$V = \sqrt{(3)}a^2 c/2 = 0.866\,a^2 c.$$

Rhombohedral:

$$V = a^3\sqrt{(1 - 3\cos^2\alpha + 2\cos^3\alpha)}.$$

Monoclinic:

$$V = abc\sin\beta.$$

A4.4 Angles between planes in cubic crystals (variants between 100 and 221)

100	100	0.00	90.00				
	110	45.00	90.00				
	111	54.74					
	210	26.56	63.43	90.00			
	211	35.26	65.90				
	221	48.19	70.53				
110	110	0.00	60.00	90.00			
	111	35.26	90.00				
	210	18.43	50.77	71.56			
	211	30.00	54.74	73.22	90.00		
	221	19.47	45.00	76.37	90.00		
111	111	0.00	70.53				
	210	39.23	75.04				
	211	19.47	61.87	90.00			
	221	15.79	54.74	78.90			
210	210	0.00	36.87	53.13	66.42	78.46	90.00
	211	24.09	43.09	56.79	79.48	90.00	
	221	26.56	41.81	53.40	63.43	72.65	90.00
211	211	0.00	33.56	48.19	60.00	70.53	80.40
	221	17.72	35.26	47.12	65.90	74.21	82.18

A4.5 Relationships between zones and planes

For a plane (hkl) which lies in a zone $[uvw]$:

$$hu + kv + lw = 0.$$

For a plane $(hkil)$ which lies in a zone $[UVTW]$:

$$hU + kV + iT + lW = 0.$$

For a lattice point with co-ordinates $[uvw]$ which lies in the nth (hkl) plane from the origin:

$$hu + kv + lw = n.$$

For a plane (hkl) which lies in the zones $[u_1 v_1 w_1]$ and $[u_2 v_2 w_2]$:

$$h = (v_1 w_2 - v_2 w_1); \quad k = (w_1 u_2 - w_2 u_1); \quad l = (u_1 v_2 - u_2 v_1).$$

For a zone $[uvw]$ which contains the planes $(h_1 k_1 l_1)$ and $(h_2 k_2 l_2)$:

$$u = (k_1 l_2 - k_2 l_1); \quad v = (l_1 h_2 - l_2 h_1); \quad w = (h_1 k_2 - h_2 k_1).$$

A4.6 Transformation matrices for trigonal crystals with rhombohedral lattices

Figure A1 shows a plan view of hexagonal layers of lattice points stacked in the rhombohedral ABC ... sequence. [See also Figure 3.3(b).] (To avoid confusion only the A hexagonal layers are outlined.) The (primitive) rhombohedral unit cell with equi-inclined lattice vectors **a, b, c** is outlined and also a unit cell of a non-primitive hexagonal unit cell with lattice vectors **A** and **B** at 120° to each other and **C** perpendicular to the plan view. Proceeding as described in Section 5.8,

$$(HKL) = (hkl) \begin{pmatrix} 1 & 0 & 1 \\ \bar{1} & 1 & 0 \\ 0 & \bar{1} & 1 \end{pmatrix}; \quad \begin{pmatrix} u \\ v \\ w \end{pmatrix} = \begin{pmatrix} 1 & 0 & 1 \\ \bar{1} & 1 & 0 \\ 0 & \bar{1} & 1 \end{pmatrix} \begin{pmatrix} U \\ V \\ W \end{pmatrix},$$

$$(hkl) = (HKL) \begin{pmatrix} \frac{2}{3} & \frac{\bar{1}}{3} & \frac{\bar{1}}{3} \\ \frac{1}{3} & \frac{1}{3} & \frac{\bar{2}}{3} \\ \frac{1}{3} & \frac{1}{3} & \frac{1}{3} \end{pmatrix}; \quad \begin{pmatrix} U \\ V \\ W \end{pmatrix} = \begin{pmatrix} \frac{2}{3} & \frac{\bar{1}}{3} & \frac{\bar{1}}{3} \\ \frac{1}{3} & \frac{1}{3} & \frac{\bar{2}}{3} \\ \frac{1}{3} & \frac{1}{3} & \frac{1}{3} \end{pmatrix} \begin{pmatrix} u \\ v \\ w \end{pmatrix},$$

where (HKL), $[UVW]$ and (hkl), $[uvw]$ refer to the Miller indices and zone axes symbols for the hexagonal and rhombohedral unit cells respectively. Note that the determinants of these two matrices are 3 and $\frac{1}{3}$ respectively, i.e. equal to the ratios of the number of lattice points in the two cells. Hence the hexagonal unit cell is known as a triple hexagonal cell because it contains three lattice points per cell. Note also that it is possible to choose the hexagonal A and B axes differently (e.g. rotated 60° to those shown in Fig. A1); this will give rhombohedral unit cells that are mirror-related, sometimes known as 'obverse' and 'reverse' unit cells.

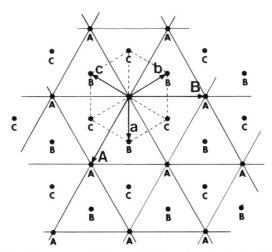

Fig. A1. A plan view of the hexagonal layers of lattice points, A, B and C, in the rhombohedral lattice. The rhombohedral unit cell and the triple hexagonal unit cell are outlined.

Appendix 5: A simple introduction to vectors and their use in crystallography

Scalars, Vectors, Tensors

In science—and, of course, everyday life—we are concerned with different types of quantities as well as quantities of the same type but of different size or magnitude. In many cases the quantities are independent of direction—mass for example, or volume or temperature. Such quantities, which can be represented by points on scales, are known as **scalars** and are denoted algebraically in familiar italic type—m for mass, t for time, x and y for unknown (scalar) quantities and so on. In many other cases, quantities are direction-dependent, or, in other words, in order to specify the quantity completely the direction as well as the magnitude of the quantity needs to be described. Such quantities are called **vectors** and are denoted albebraically in printing by bold type—**a**, **b**, **x**, **y**, etc. In handwriting an underlining is substituted for bold type, i.e. a, b, x, y, etc.

Velocity is an everyday example of a vector quantity—we need to specify not only the speed of an object but the direction in which it is travelling. A motor car travelling 50 km h^{-1} due north has the same speed as a motor car travelling 50 km h^{-1} due east, but their velocities are different—one has a velocity of 50 km h^{-1} *north* and the other has a velocity of 50 km h^{-1} *east*. The velocities may be represented as vectors by arrows—one pointing north and one pointing east. The lengths of the arrows or vectors gives the speed—the greater the speed the longer the arrows. In the above case (50 km h^{-1}), the arrows are of equal length.

Heat and electrical current flow, electrical and magnetic fields are examples of vector quantities of interest in crystal physics, but in geometrical crystallography we are invariably concerned with vectors which denote displacements: for example the displacement from one corner of a unit cell to the next, or the displacement from one atom to another. Crystal axes or directions are examples of such displacement vector quantities. In Fig. 5.1 (p. 55) the directions and lengths of the edges of the unit cell are all denoted by the vectors **a**, **b**, and **c**. In the special case of cubic crystals (Fig. 3.1, p. 35) these vectors are all at 90° (orthogonal) and are also the same length, but they are **not** identical vectors because they 'point' in different directions.

The 'length' of a vector is called its **modulus**. In the case of the motor car the modulus of the velocity is the speed. The modulus of a vector is written in two ways, either in italic type, *a*, (denoting that it is a scalar quantity) or with the heavy type vector symbol bracketed between straight vertical lines thus: $|\mathbf{a}|$. Hence $|\mathbf{a}| = a$.

In Fig. 3.1 the moduli *a*, *b*, and *c* of the unit cell vectors for the fourteen Bravais lattices are indicated. In the case of cubic (and rhombohedral) crystals, the unit cell edge lengths, or moduli, are all identical and are represented (for all three axes) by *a*. Hence $|\mathbf{a}| = |\mathbf{b}| = |\mathbf{c}| = a$ (as in Fig. 3.1).

Scalars and vectors are particular types of quantities which are known in general as **tensors**. There are other, more complicated types of tensors which are of importance in crystal physics because they are able to describe properties such as conductivity or stress which vary not only with the direction of the applied field or force but also with the orientation of the crystal. 'Everyday' examples of tensors (other than scalars or vectors) are not easy to provide, but the following, perhaps rather contrived example, may illustrate the ideas involved.

Consider rain-water flowing down a corrugated roof. The flow of water (a vector) is obviously down the roof, parallel to the corrugations and parallel also to a vector representing the inclined component of the gravitational field. The effective 'conductivity' may simply be regarded as the quantity that relates these two parallel vectors. Now consider a (badly made) roof in which the corrugations are set at an angle. The water will partly run sideways, along the 'preferred direction' of the corrugations and will partly flow downwards over from one corrugation to the next. The overall water flow will lie in a direction somewhere between the lines of the corrugations and downwards. In this case the effective gravitational field vector and the water flow vector are not parallel, and in estimating the effective conductivity of the roof, both the 'downwards' and 'sideways' components of the water flow need to be taken into account.

In crystals the 'corrugations' may be loosely regarded as preferred or easy directions of, say, heat or electrical flow. The conductivity of the crystal is the quantity which relates one vector (heat or electrical flow) to another vector (temperature or electrical field gradient). As indicated in the example above these vectors may not, except in special cases, be parallel and in general a total of 9 terms or components* are required in order to specify the conductivity completely.

Conductivity is called a second-rank tensor property. There are, in addition, third-rank tensor properties (e.g. piezo-electricity) which are specified by 27 components and fourth-rank tensor properties (e.g. elasticity) which are specified by 81 components. Scalars, which are

---

*These components are not all independent: their number is greatly reduced by symmetry considerations. For further information on tensors, see J. F. Nye *Physical Properties of Crystals*, Clarendon Press, Oxford, 1957, Second Edition 1982, and F. G. Fumi *Il Nuovo Cimento* (1952) Volume 9, pp. 739–56.

specified by 1 term or component are, in this classification, called zero-rank tensors and vectors which are, as shown below, specified by 3 components are called first-rank tensors.

Resolving vectors into components and vector addition

Consider the (displacement) vector **r** drawn in Fig. A2 which is outlined in a (two-dimensional) lattice with unit cell vectors **a** and **b**. Note that all these vectors have a common origin.

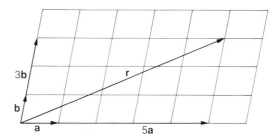

Fig. A2.

The vector **r** may be resolved into its components in the directions of the unit cell vectors **a** and **b**. These components, 5**a** and 3**b**, are drawn in Fig. A2. Added together they give **r**, i.e. **r** = 5**a** + 3**b**.

In vector analysis in general, cubic or Cartesian axes are chosen, and the unit cell vectors are labelled **i**, **j**, **k** rather than **a**, **b**, **c**. Also, the moduli of **i**, **j**, **k** are unity and they are known as **unit vectors**. The general symbol for a unit vector is **n**, i.e. $|\mathbf{n}| = 1$.

Multiplying vectors—scalar products and vector products

There are two ways in which vectors can be multiplied, namely, the scalar product and the vector product, the general significance of which go beyond the scope of this book. We will consider only the multiplication of displacement vectors.

The scalar (or 'dot') product, **a·b** may be thought of as 'representing' the product of the moduli of the vectors resolved in the direction of one or other of the vectors. For example (Fig. A3), if the angle between the vectors, drawn from a common origin, is θ, the resolved component of the modulus of **b** along the **a** direction is $b \cos \theta$. Hence **a·b** = $ab \cos \theta$. The same result applies if **a** is resolved along the direction of **b**.

If one of the vectors is a unit vector—say in Fig. A3 **a** = **n**, then the scalar product **n·b** = $b \cos \theta$ (since $|\mathbf{n}| = 1$): it is simply the modulus of **b** resolved along the direction of the unit vector **n**. The scalar product may therefore be

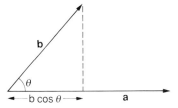

Fig. A3.

thought of as a 'shorthand' means of resolving the vectors along different directions.

Clearly, the maximum value of the scalar product occurs when the vectors are parallel ($\theta = 0°$) and the minimum value, zero, occurs when they are at right angles ($\theta = 90°$).

The vector (or 'cross') product $\mathbf{a} \times \mathbf{b}$ may be thought of as 'representing' the area outlined by two vectors. In Fig. A4 the area outlined by the vectors $\mathbf{a}$ and $\mathbf{b}$ is $ab \sin \theta$. But there is more: the area may represent a crystal plane or surface, the **orientation** of which also needs to be specified. The orientation of the surface may be specified by a direction normal to it, i.e. perpendicular to the page. Let the unit vector along this direction be $\mathbf{n}$; then $\mathbf{a} \times \mathbf{b} = (ab \sin \theta)\mathbf{n}$.

Fig. A4.

In general, the vector product is expressed as $\mathbf{a} \times \mathbf{b} = \mathbf{c}$, where $\mathbf{c}$ is perpendicular to $\mathbf{a}$ and $\mathbf{b}$ and $|\mathbf{c}| = ab \sin \theta$. The largest value of $\mathbf{c}$ occurs when $\mathbf{a}$ and $\mathbf{b}$ are at right angles and the smallest value, zero, occurs when they are parallel. Finally, the vector product involves the use of a sign convention: the vector $\mathbf{c}$ or $\mathbf{n}$ is perpendicular to the plane defined by $\mathbf{a}$ and $\mathbf{b}$ but can have one of two directions, i.e. with reference to Fig. A4, it can be 'up' from the page or 'down'. One vector must have a + sign and the opposite must have a − sign. The sign convention is as follows. Consider in Fig. A4 an (ordinary) right-handed screw coming out of the page (i.e. parallel to $\mathbf{c}$ or $\mathbf{n}$) through the common origin of $\mathbf{a}$ and $\mathbf{b}$. If we 'screw' from $\mathbf{a}$ to $\mathbf{b}$ the screw will move 'upwards' and this upwards direction is the direction or sense of $\mathbf{c}$. If we screw in the opposite direction, from $\mathbf{b}$ to $\mathbf{a}$, the screw will move downwards.

Hence, the order of the multiplication of vectors is important and leads to the **anticommunicative law** for the vector product:

$$\mathbf{a} \times \mathbf{b} = - (\mathbf{b} \times \mathbf{a}).$$

Multiplication of vectors in terms of components

Calculations are generally made easier if vectors are expressed in terms of their components on a Cartesian axis system with unit vectors, **i, j, k** at right angles. In this case $\mathbf{i \cdot j} = 1, \mathbf{i \cdot j} = 0, \mathbf{i} \times \mathbf{i} = 0, \mathbf{i} \times \mathbf{j} = \mathbf{k}$, and similarly for the other combinations of **i, j** and **k**.

Writing

$$\mathbf{a} = (a_1\mathbf{i} + a_2\mathbf{j} + a_3\mathbf{k}) \text{ and } \mathbf{b} = (b_1\mathbf{i} + b_2\mathbf{j} + b_3\mathbf{k})$$

the scalar product

$$\begin{aligned}\mathbf{a \cdot b} &= (a_1\mathbf{i} + a_2\mathbf{j} + a_3\mathbf{k}) \cdot (b_1\mathbf{i} + b_2\mathbf{j} + b_3\mathbf{k}) \\ &= a_1 b_1 \mathbf{i \cdot i} + a_1 b_2 \mathbf{i \cdot j} + \ldots\ldots \\ &= (a_1 b_1 + a_2 b_2 + a_3 b_3)\end{aligned}$$

(all the other terms cancel because $\mathbf{i \cdot i} = 1$ and $\mathbf{i \cdot j} = 0$, etc.)

the vector product

$$\begin{aligned}\mathbf{a} \times \mathbf{b} &= (a_1\mathbf{i} + a_2\mathbf{j} + a_3\mathbf{k}) \times (b_1\mathbf{i} + b_2\mathbf{j} + b_3\mathbf{k}) \\ &= a_1 b_1 (\mathbf{i} \times \mathbf{i}) + a_1 b_2 (\mathbf{i} \times \mathbf{j}) + \ldots\ldots \\ &= (a_2 b_3 - b_2 a_3)\mathbf{i} + (a_3 b_1 - b_3 a_1)\mathbf{j} + (a_1 b_2 - b_1 a_2)\mathbf{k}\end{aligned}$$

(all the other terms cancel because $\mathbf{i} \times \mathbf{i} = 0$ and $\mathbf{i} \times \mathbf{j} = \mathbf{k}$ etc.).

The vector product may be expressed in matrix form as a determinant:

$$\mathbf{a} \times \mathbf{b} = \begin{vmatrix} \mathbf{i} & \mathbf{j} & \mathbf{k} \\ a_1 & a_2 & a_3 \\ b_1 & b_2 & b_3 \end{vmatrix} .$$

Volumes of unit cells in vector notation

The volume of a unit cell defined by vectors **a, b,** and **c** is 'the area of the base times the height'.

The 'area of the base' is $(\mathbf{a} \times \mathbf{b}) = (ab \sin \theta)\mathbf{n}$. The 'height' is the component of **c** resolved in the direction of the normal **n** (Fig. A5), i.e. the height $= \mathbf{n \cdot c} = c \cos \phi$. Hence the volume $V = (\mathbf{a} \times \mathbf{b}) \cdot \mathbf{c}$. It is a scalar quantity. The vectors **a, b, c** in this equation may be 'cycled' but the sequence must be maintained, i.e.

$$V = (\mathbf{a} \times \mathbf{b}) \cdot \mathbf{c} = \mathbf{a} \cdot (\mathbf{b} \times \mathbf{c}) = (\mathbf{c} \times \mathbf{a}) \cdot \mathbf{b} \text{ etc.}$$

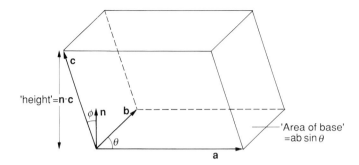

Fig. A5.

If the sequence is reversed, i.e. $(\mathbf{b} \times \mathbf{a}) \cdot \mathbf{c}$, then a negative volume results. In practice this can occur if a left-handed set of axes are substituted, inadvertently or otherwise, for a right-handed set.

The reciprocal unit cell $\mathbf{a}^*$, $\mathbf{b}^*$, $\mathbf{c}^*$ can be derived from the 'direct' unit cell $\mathbf{a}$, $\mathbf{b}$, $\mathbf{c}$ in a similar way as outlined in Section 6.4.4 (page 75). Note that the relationships

$$\mathbf{a}^* = \frac{\mathbf{b} \times \mathbf{c}}{V} \quad \text{etc.}$$

are valid for the primitive unit cells for any axis system.

Answers to exercises

Chapter 1

3(a). In the ccp structure there are four sets of close-packed planes and six close-packed directions and in hcp only one set of close-packed planes and three close-packed directions.

3(b). In the bcc structure there are six sets of closest-packed planes and four close-packed directions.

4. In the ccp structure each close-packed plane contains three close-packed directions, i.e. three slip systems share a common close-packed plane. As there are four sets of close-packed planes in the ccp structure there are therefore twelve slip systems. In the bcc structure each closest-packed plane contains two close-packed directions, i.e. two slip systems share a common closest-packed plane. As there are six sets of closest-packed planes in the bcc structure there are therefore also twelve slip systems.

5. The height of the tetrahedron (i.e. the distance from its vertex to its base) is simply $\sqrt{(2/3)}$ of the length of its edge which is the unit cell edge length a.
   Hence

$$c/a = 2\sqrt{(2/3)} = 1.633.$$

Chapter 2

2. The lattice type is $p3m1$ (refer to your drawings or question 1).

3. The lattice type is pg. The glide lines run vertically through the back heels of the black men and the raised hands of the white men.

4(a). A diad at the centre of the board and two diagonal mirror lines.

4(b). A diad only.

Chapter 3

1. (a) is orthorhombic C; (b) is not a Bravais lattice because the points *do not* all have an identical environment [see the two-dimensional examples, Figures 2.2(b) and (c)]; (c) is orthorhombic P (two primitive cells are drawn together).

2. (a) is orthorhombic P (relocate the origin at $x'y'z'$); (b) is orthorhombic I (relocate the origin at $0\frac{1}{2}0$); (c) is orthorhombic C (relocate the origin at $00z'$; the motif is two atoms, one of each type).

Chapter 4

2.

Structure	*Bravais lattice*	*Motif*
NaCl	Cubic F	(Na and Cl)
CsCl	Cubic P	(Cs and Cl)
ZnS (sphalerite)	Cubic F	(Zn and S)
ZnS (wurtzite)	Hexagonal P	(2Zn + 2S)
Li_2O (or CaF_2)	Cubic F	(2Li + 1O)
$CaTiO_3$	Cubic P	(1Ca, 1Ti, 3O)

Chapter 5

1. In fcc slip planes are $\{111\}$, slip directions are $\langle 110 \rangle$.
   In bcc slip planes are $\{110\}$, slip directions are $\langle 111 \rangle$.
2. $[23\bar{1}]$, i.e. $2.1 + 3.1 + \bar{1}.5 = 0$.
   (321), i.e. $3.1 + 2.\bar{1} + 1.\bar{1} = 0$.
3. Triclinic, none; monoclinic, (010) and $[010]$; tetragonal, (001) and $[001]$; $(hk0)$ and $[hk0]$.
4. $(4\bar{1}\bar{1})$; $(\bar{2}31)$; $[\bar{1}2,11\bar{4}]$; $[3\bar{3}1]$ [or, their opposites, e.g. $(\bar{4}11)$, etc.].
5. (a) $d_{101} = 375$ pm; $d_{100} = 452$ pm; $d_{111} = 302$ pm; $d_{202} = 188$ pm.
   (b) $\alpha = 48.1°$; $\beta = 53.5°$; $\gamma = 63.4°$.
   (c) $p = 61.8°$; $q = 58.0°$; $r = 45.3°$.
   α, β, γ are not identical to p, q, r because the (111) plane normal is not parallel to the $[111]$ direction in orthorhombic crystals. These directions are only parallel in the case of cubic crystals.
6. $[001] = [0001]$; $[010] = [\bar{1}2\bar{1}0]$; $[210] = [30\bar{3}0] = [10\bar{1}0]$; $[110] = [11\bar{2}0]$.

Chapter 6

1. These reciprocal lattice sections all consist of hexagonal arrays of recriprocal lattice points, those closest to the origin representing the $\{10\bar{1}0\}$ planes (hexagonal lattice), $\{110\}$ planes (cubic *I* lattice) and $\{220\}$ planes (cubic *F* lattice).
2. Check your answers with the equations given in Appendix 4.
3. Yes.

Chapter 7

1. $d_{110} = 0.2027$ nm; $d_{200} = 0.1433$ nm; and $d_{211} = 0.1170$ nm. Planes whose d-spacings are smaller than $\lambda/2$ ($= 0.1146$ nm) do not satisfy Bragg's Law since the maximum possible value of θ is 90°.
2. The zone axis of the pattern is $\langle 112 \rangle$. The particular variant obtained depends upon the variants of the indices chosen to index the pattern consistently.
3. Bragg's law is satisfied for the planes $(2\bar{2}0)$, $(3\bar{1}0)$, (400), (310), (220) (in the $hk0$ section); $(4\bar{1}1)$, $(4\bar{1}\bar{1})$, (301), (411), $(41\bar{1})$ (in the $hk1$ and $hk\bar{1}$ sections) and $(3\bar{1}2)$, $(3\bar{1}\bar{2})$, (202), $(20\bar{2})$, (312), $(31\bar{2})$ (in the $hk2$ and $hk\bar{2}$ sections). The (larger) reflecting sphere does not extend beyond the $hk2$ and $hk\bar{2}$ sections.
4. Bragg's law is satisfied for the planes (420), $(4\bar{2}0)$, (220) and $(2\bar{2}0)$.

Further reading

Books which largely cover the subject-matter in this handbook.

Buerger, M. J. (1971). *Introduction to Crystal Geometry*. McGraw-Hill, New York.

Glazer, A. M. (1987). *The Structures of Crystals*. Adam Hilger, Bristol.

Kennon, N. F. (1978). *Patterns in Crystals*. John Wiley, New York.

Phillips, F. C. (1977). *Introduction to Crystallography* (3rd edn). Longmans, London.

Steadman, R. (1982). *Crystallography*. Van Nostrand Reinhold, Wokingham.

Windle, A. (1977). *A First Course in Crystallography*. G. Bell and Sons Ltd, London.

Books which contain chapters on introductory crystallography but in which the main emphasis is on the crystallography of X-ray and/or electron diffraction, crystal chemistry, mineralogy, materials science, crystalline defects, etc.

Azároff, L. V. (1968). *Elements of X-ray Crystallography*. McGraw-Hill, New York.

Barrett, C. S. and Massalski, T. B. (1980). *The structure of metals* (3rd edn). Pergamon, Oxford.

Brown, P. J. and Forsyth, J. B. (1973). *The crystal structure of solids*. Arnold, London.

Buerger, M. J. (1970). *Contemporary Crystallography*. McGraw-Hill, New York.

Bunn, C. W (1967). *Chemical Crystallography* (2nd edn). Oxford University Press, Oxford.

Cullity, B. D. (1978). *Elements of X-Ray Diffraction* (2nd edn). Addison–Wesley, Reading, MA.

Dyson, D. J., Andrews, K. W., and Keown, S. R. (1971). *Interpretation of Electron Diffraction Patterns* (2nd edn). Hilger & Watts, London.

Edington, J. W. (1975). *Electron Diffraction in the Electron Microscope. Monograph* 2. Practical Electron Microscopy in Materials Science. Philips Technical Library. Macmillan, London.

Evans, R. C. (1964). *An Introduction to Crystal Chemistry* (2nd edn). Cambridge University Press, Cambridge.

Hecht, E. and Zajak, A. (1987). *Optics* (2nd edn). Addison-Wesley, London.

Henry, N. F. M., Lipson, H. and Wooster, W. A. (1961). *The Interpretation of X-ray Diffraction Photographs* (2nd edn). MacMillan, New York.

Jenkins, F. A. and White, H. E. (1976). *Fundamentals of Optics* (4th edn). McGraw-Hill, New York.

Kelly, A. and Groves, G. W. (1970). *Crystallography and Crystal Defects*. Longman, London.

McKie, D. and McKie, C. (1986). *Essentials of Crystallography*. Blackwell Scientific Publications, Oxford.

Nye, J. F. (1985). Physical Properties of Crystals: Their Representation by Tensors and Matrices. Oxford University Press, Oxford.

Smith, J. V. (1978). *Geometrical and Structural Crystallography*. John Wiley, New York.

Taylor, C. A. (1978). *Images: a Unified View of Diffraction and Image Formation with all Kinds of Radiation.* Wykeham Publications, London and Basingstoke.

Thomas, G. and Goringe, M. J. (1979). *Transmission Electron Microscopy of Materials.* Wiley, Chichester and New York.

Verma, A. R. and Srivastava, O. N. (1982). *Crystallography for Solid State Physics.* Wiley Eastern, New Delhi.

Wells, A. F. (1968). *The Third Dimension in Chemistry.* Clarendon Press, Oxford.

Whittaker, E. J. W. (1981). *Crystallography for Earth Science (and other solid state) Students.* Pergamon, Oxford.

Books of general or historical interest:

Bragg, W. H. and Bragg, W. L. (1966). *The Crystalline State*, Vol. 1. G. Bell and Sons Ltd, London.

Although this book was first published over 50 years ago, it remained in print until recently and is still invaluable for its clarity and simplicity.

Ewald, P. P. and Numerous Crystallographers (1962). *Fifty Years of X-ray Diffraction.* Published for the International Union of Crystallography, by N. V. A. Oosthoek's Uitgeversmaatschappij, Utrecht.

An invaluable source-book which describes the beginnings of X-ray diffraction, the growing field and development of schools of crystallography throughout the world, and the personal reminiscences and memoirs of those who participated. One of the strongest impressions is that of an international community of scientists which transcended the barriers of nationality, politics and war.

MacGillavry, C. H. (1976). *Symmetry Aspects of M. C. Escher's Periodic Drawings* (2nd edn). Published for the International Union of Crystallography by Bohn, Scheltema & Holkema, Utrecht.

Superb illustrations with clear descriptive analyses. The notion of colour symmetry is also included.

Watson, J. D. (1968). *The Double Helix: A Personal Account of the Discovery of the Structure of DNA.* With a Foreword by Sir Lawrence Bragg. Weidenfield & Nicholson, London, and Penguin Books, Harmondsworth (1970).

Index

Note: Illustrations are indicated by italic page numbers.

129